FARAWAY THUNDER

A Journey through Army Life & the Gulf War

CAREY JONES

FARAWAY THUNDER
A Journey through Army Life & the Gulf War

2ⁿᵈ Printing February, 2000

ISBN 0-9672615-0-3

Library of Congress Catalog Card Number: 99-95120

Printed in the United States of America

For additional information please contact the publisher.

VISTA PUBLISHING
523 1ˢᵀ St W.
Zumbrota, MN 55992
1 888 262 2925

AUTHOR'S NOTE

I have to thank Phillip Wynn, who's encouragement and editing during the first two drafts of the manuscript helped me immeasurably. Phil's fascination with the Gulf War and his continual requests of me to tell these stories started this whole process. It wasn't long before he convinced me I could write them all down.

I debated long and hard over the language in various parts of the book. I've gone in to take out words or phrases I thought were too graphic, only to go back later to re-add them if I thought they added to the characters or the reality of the story. The language is not intended to offend anyone.

The events in the book are my recollections as they occurred. As with anyones memory, mine is nowhere near perfect, though every conversation in the book took place in one form or another and the dates and times are, with some research and looking back through letters, accurate. The characters are all real people, though most names are changed.

Lastly, I want to thank my family. Their support has always been there for me.

Any mistakes are mine.

DEDICATION

To the memory of Staff Sergeant Roy J. Summerall; so as not to be forgotten.

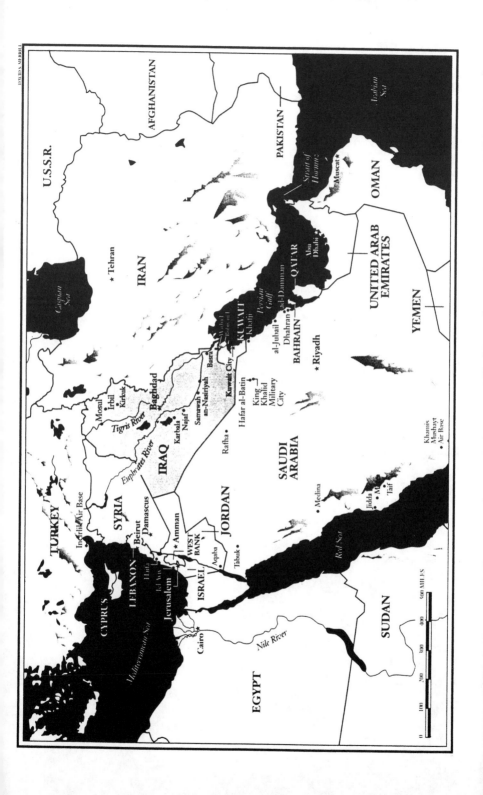

Prologue

We crossed the Neutral Zone at 1621 hours yesterday afternoon. We traveled a good part of last night and all day today through this part of Iraq. It is desolate here, absolutely nothing in sight for miles ... I can't believe the rain. Isn't this supposed to be the desert? There are no windows in any of our vehicles and driving this humvee through the rain without the damn windows is no fun. I guess the enemy can see the sun glaring off windshields from a great distance, but hell, the sun hasn't shown for two weeks! How could there be any glare?

I keep worrying about this damn broken-down air force hummer. Just how did I end up driving an air force humvee? There's a good story. The air defense guys attached to my unit drove the thing over a cliff bending both front wheels to the outside of the vehicle. It sat around the maintenance area at least a month waiting for parts. When the parts didn't arrive and the war was about to start the mechanics decided to heat the torsion bars and bend the wheels straight. We never really told the air force their vehicle is fixed; technically it's not. You see, our high speed decision makers at battalion HQ figure a lowly couple of commo guys don't really need a vehicle. Sergeant T's been pissed about this for months. I've got to calm him down about every other day when he finds out we've got 18 radios to transport to higher maintenance and no vehicle to get them there. That's been my main mission; keeping Sergeant T from tearing somebody's head off at battalion. Anyway, we just loaded this humvee and started driving it. Everybody keeps quiet about it around the air force boys. They think the thing is still parked back in the desert somewhere. So the wheels mechanic who heated the torsion bars and bent them straight says it's in good shape. He tells me not to drive faster than 35. He's not sure what would happen if those bars decided to give.

We drove a hundred miles today and didn't see anything. No towns, no people, no animals, nothing. Just this desert weed; like sagebrush but not quite. The sand and hard rock like crust of this place remind me of pictures I saw from Apollo moon-shots when I was a kid. Total desolation.

We stopped for the night at 2100 hours. It's 0030 hours now and the shelling to our south keeps me awake. The artillery bombardment from that area has been incessant. I can't imagine how much lead, steel, and shrapnel we must be dropping on those guys. I pity anyone in its path. I can occasionally see flashes of light from explosions as the shells and missiles hit their targets. The ground shakes. I guess they are 20, maybe 30 klicks to our south, though I can't be sure.

Sergeant T is sleeping on the hood of the hummer. We took one of the tents in the back and draped it over the top of the vehicle down to the front of the hood. He climbed through the non-existent windows and laid out his bag. I sleep across the front seats. With my softer gear underneath for padding it's somewhat comfortable. I crank up the vehicle now and then to get some heat out to the front of the hood, the

2

only advantage I can see to having no windows. 40 degrees and rain. What kind of desert is this? I begin to think about how it is that a college boy like myself ends up in the army, driving a broken down air force humvee, in the middle of a desert fighting a war. Wouldn't any reasonably bright person be somewhere else? These are good questions. I guess I've got time to think about them. The shelling isn't slowing. A far-off incessant rolling storm, distant and pounding, almost comforting. Like faraway thunder on a dark summer's night; only the thunder is manmade.

I won't be sleeping any time soon.

Part 1

Chapter 1
The Army?

"The army is for you, guy. Believe me, man, there ain't a better thing you can do. Hey look, three hots and a cot. At least that's always gonna be there."

"Listen, Tim. Going into the army has never even crossed my mind. Well, maybe it has, but never seriously."

"The army is a great place to get a start ya know."

"You sound like one of those recruiting commercials."

"What I'm saying is look what it did for me."

"They kicked you out back in 69."

"Yeah, but that was beyond my control. I was 19, going to Vietnam, and it scared the hell out of me. I saw my friend come back all shot to hell. They put him in a VA hospital. After I saw that, no way."

"But you were a green beret, the best, fearless. My best friend is a green beret, I know what those guys go through."

"I trained for one year in special forces. Just because they trained me was I suppose to go off and get shot up or killed? You know how many SF guys got it in Nam? Wasn't in the cards, bud."

"So you're tellin' me that after going to college all these years I should go ahead and give my education to Uncle Sam? Man, you're way out there."

"Yeah, but do you know what you want to do with that schooling? The way you talk to me about the economy and the job market, things don't sound so good. Hey guy, three hots and a cot. I'm tellin' ya. It's 1984, and how long's this recession been goin' on? Ronald Reagan says we're out of it. I don't see it, man, no way."

"Yeah, it looks pretty tough to me. I figure if I get on with somebody and the economy goes belly up, I'm out there. Last hired first fired, or somethin' like that."

"Go talk to a recruiter, bud. You never know, he might have something great for you. Check out infantry. You can't beat it. I mean the challenge is incredible."

"Sure buddy, infantry."

I can't say Tim Jones was right, or that he talked me into the army. I went to see that recruiter and did this guy have a job for me! Four months later I was in basic training crawling through the mud. I got a good army job; at least everybody from my recruiter to the guys processing me into the army said it was a good job. The title had six, long, hard-to-remember words in it, which I never did memorize. I did ask my recruiter what this job was about. He didn't quite exactly know. It had something to do with high-tech communications, and hey, any job with six words in the title, some of which neither one of us could pronounce, must be pretty damn good. Other things got thrown in there like officer candidate school, and paying off my student loans. My recruiters best advice was "Go for it!" Hey, it did sound good and what did I have to lose? I was young. Three years; no time at all. I went for it.

So there I was, in South Carolina someplace. I'm a Midwestern boy, brought up in the north where it's cold. But South Carolina in January has to be the coldest place I've ever been. Lying in the mud and firing my M-16 is what I remember most about basic .... and cold. But I made it. I guess I had a pretty good idea of what to expect, though I hadn't seen anything about this great job I was supposed to have. My drill sergeant wasn't worried about fancy high-tech jobs. He was there to turn us into soldiers, plain and simple. The rest of us had a better term for it. Grunts. I guess no matter how far a person goes in the army, or what he or she ends up doing for the army, his or her first and foremost job is to get out in the dirt, or the woods, and tote an M-16. Really, I guess I knew that about the army, too. The television commercials about all the great jobs the army has to offer are, for the most part, true, but there is always a price. With the army it's learning to be a grunt. Every person in the army, no matter their primary job, has something referred to as a secondary specialty. It's called 11 Bravo; Infantry. Plain and simple.

After basic I started training for the fancy job the army had given me, and it was pretty good. I liked the guys, and girls, I was working with. But I was worried. An event some four months in the past had me in that state of mind. That event happened my second day of basic training, the day I was informed exactly what the high-tech job with six unpronounceable words in the title was all about ....

I had just had all my hair cut off and someone grabbed me saying I had a briefing of some kind. In the briefing room were two females sitting at school desks watching television. I sat and watched with them thinking how lucky I was to be watching TV in basic. An hour later a man wearing a long beige trench coat with a high collar came in, swaggered up to a podium with some type of federal agency stamp on it, then stood behind the podium for approximately one full minute staring at us. Finally, he pulled a very nondescript US Government Skilcraft pen from the inside of his trench coat, which he never did take off, and stated: "This pen is a weapon!"

Now, the first few days of basic training are a little mind bending. Drill sergeants with very loud voices are shuffling you here and there for shots and records and clothing; a lot of pushups got thrown in there somewhere. But never in my wildest dreams did I imagine being lectured on the tactical abilities of a ball-point pen. He claimed he was

7

with some government agency I'd never heard of and that for this high-tech job we needed a top secret, sensitive compartmented information access, security clearance. That certainly sounded important, but what it was I could only speculate. He then spent the next three hours telling us exactly what our high-tech job was all about, with most of the explanation centering on Soviet KGB agents, who he said already had our names because we'd signed up for this job. He added that he knew none of us had been totally truthful about our backgrounds. If a KGB agent knew something about us that we hadn't told our government, we could be blackmailed to give information to the KGB; information we would learn doing our high-tech job. When he finished I was white as a sheet.

He took us one at a time into a smaller room adjacent to the room with the podium. There he had a questionnaire for me to fill out. The questionnaire asked if I'd ever smoked marijuana? "Well, yeah. I'd smoked it a few times. I went to college in the 70's you know." Had I ever been arrested? "Well, yeah. It was for misdemeanor possession of a thimbleful of pot." Had I ever mooned anybody? "Well, yeah. It happened back in high school." A harmless prank I thought. After I'd filled out the questionnaire the trench coat asked me a few questions about it, then said someone would be back in touch with me.

So there I was, four months after my encounter with the trench coat, in the ninth week of training for the fancy high-tech job, when a letter came down telling me that due to inconsistencies, or minor indiscretions, in my background, I would be denied the security clearance I needed. The inconsistency came about from my not having told the whole truth during an initial security screening for the high-tech job. During that screening, which happened about three months before I started basic, I'd seen no good reason to tell anyone I'd ever smoked pot, or been arrested six years earlier as a teenager and fined 50 dollars for possession. Of course, this was well before I'd found out KGB agents would be tailing me through the streets of Berlin ....

So I was out of the high-tech job. Two months later I was out of the army. I wanted to stay in and would have taken a less high-tech job to do that. An army lawyer and I put them through two months of paperwork before they were legally able to put me out. My battalion commander didn't believe I would take a lesser job to stay in the army; something about my ending up a cook. Private First Class Jones, now ex-PFC Jones, was out on the street.

Maybe the army wasn't the best thing for me to do after college.

Chapter 2
The Real World

I suppose I could have been bitter about what had happened to me in the army. I mean, how many guys with a college degree get kicked out of the army? But then, life goes on. Being bitter wasn't going to get me a job.

So I found a job and all in all it wasn't bad. I was hired as a manager trainee with a big hardware chain in Minneapolis. When the personnel man who hired me explained the company he said they were 106 years old and would be there tomorrow.

I liked working in the hardware business. I grew up on a farm, so I knew all about hardware. I'd sell a little drainpipe here, some nails there. Real solid type work the way I looked at it. It would make me feel good to help an old lady match some stain with the color of her woodwork. Nothing extraordinary, just solid down-to-earth type business. It wasn't long before I was promoted to assistant manager and moved to a little suburban store. The company had 30 stores in all. A guy could go places with a company that big.

Pretty soon a year went by, then another six months. Things were going real well at the little suburban hardware store until, well .... my district manager explained it like this: "The company's been sold and your store's gonna be closed, son. Looks like we got about a year before it all goes down, till then ...."

"This is the company that's 106 years old," I said. "How can they just up and shut it down?"

"It's hard times for small stores like ours. There's a lot of competition from the big discount chains .... Sorry, son."

So I had a year to find something new and I was sure something good would come along .... Three months later I was standing in front of an army recruiting office.

It crossed my mind that fate had led me there. Then again, maybe I was just plain nuts. Maybe I'm a glutton for punishment. Why the hell else would I put myself back in the army after what had happened to me the first time? I went in, sat down in front of the recruiter's desk, and spilled my guts about my first experience with the army. One hour later he told me I had a 90 to 95% chance of getting back in.

"Even after all the terrible things I've done?"

"Son, we can put you back in the army. Make you lean and mean again."

"I'll have to think about it a little while. I came down here to find out just what kind of choices I have."

"Listen, I can get you back in the army and probably get you a pretty darn good job."

"Where have I heard that before?"

"What'd you say, son?"

"Ahh, nothing. I was just thinking out loud."

"Go home and think about it, then give me a call. What you done here, as far as what happened in the army, I've seen worse. It's really not that bad."

"You really think so?"

"Sure guy. Go home and sleep on it. Then give me a call."

I did go home and sleep on it. There were a lot of reasons, in my thinking, to go back into the army. First and foremost is that it's damn hard to go to an employer and tell them you were in the army only six months. When you tell somebody that the wheels start turning in their heads. I could see them thinking, "Yeah, this guy couldn't hack it." That drove me crazy.

Like I said, I grew up in the midwest, a little town in southeastern Minnesota. It's the type of place Sinclair Lewis wrote about, or Garrison Keillor still writes about. Everybody knew everybody else's business. Being from a small town and school gave me a lot of opportunity to excel at a lot of different things. I played football, basketball, and baseball; played drums in the band, sang in the choir, acted in all the school plays. I even managed to get good grades. The Future Farmers of America were my peers. Yeah, I'd built a reputation in my hometown and it was a good one. In their eyes I was a good kid with potential. I had pressure on me from those people in my hometown. I felt I had to do good. Getting kicked out of the army seemed to shoot that all to hell.

In small town America the military has respect like nothing else. Memorial Day is probably the best example. There's a parade and people march to the cemetery to remember all the dead war heroes from my little town. The military is like a religion among the old Legionnaires who march in that parade. I had gone into the military and messed up. Dealing with people in my home town after that was tough, the toughest thing I've ever done. I do know now that the pressure I put on myself was of my own making. No one told me directly that I'd let them down, which would have been a pretty stupid thing to say to me anyway; hell, it's my life. I alone felt I had done something wrong. Though nothing was said, I still felt the pressure; small town peer pressure I guess. It is one hell of a motivational force. A motivational force to do the right thing.

Going back into the army, then, and serving a couple of years honorably was the best thing I could do. I had to prove to myself, my hometown, and my country, that I could hack it. Sure I'd made some mistakes in the past, but I'd show them just exactly what I was made of. I'd prove that I came from good stock and that my hardworking midwestern farm boy upbringing was worth something. Yes, I would show them and the army that I could pull myself up by my bootstraps! Be all that I could be!

"So, you want to come back in to the green machine?"

"You bet, Sergeant. At first I was thinking of the reserves, but if you can get me a two year stint and Europe, I'll go full time."

"Oh sure. I can get you two years and Europe. A full time enlistment is the only way to go, buddy. I'll have you shinin' boots and wearing jungle green in no time."

My recruiter was wrong on two of the three counts. None of this two year stuff. The army said four years or nothing. Second, getting right in was way off the mark. It took eight months of paperwork. I had to have six personal references. I called on everyone from old high school teachers to employers I hadn't worked for in years. Uncle Sam wanted to know everything I had ever done and just about everyone I had ever known. They wanted to know every police infraction I had ever received right down to parking tickets. Because my recruiter had done such a good job finding all that information and organizing it, he was promoted!

Well, eight months and a mountain of paperwork later, I found out I'd passed the test. All the skeletons in my closet had been aired and in the end the army found out I was just who I told them I was. I took the four year enlistment figuring the army was getting even with me. I mean, they must have spent an enormous sum of money checking out who I am. I got the tour in Europe, having always wanted to see it, and a job in communications (albeit a little less high-tech this time) troubleshooting plain old radios that are in tactical vehicles like tanks and jeeps. The whole job was even explained to me before I went in. No problem.

It was May of 1988 and I was at the processing center raising my hand. I swore to support and defend the Constitution of the United States against all enemies, foreign and domestic. Standing there giving the oath that day in 1988, I could never have foreseen that in the near future I would see the Mideast in flames, up close and personal.

Chapter 3
Germany

Within four months I was in a place called Kirch-Gons, West Germany. I was assigned to a unit in the 3rd Armored Division and stationed at a place called the Rock, right outside Kirch-Gons. The Rock was exactly what its name implied. It sat on a hilltop surrounded by open German countryside. Its reputation held it as one of the toughest tours in Germany. When I arrived and people told me just how bad a place the Rock was, I figured it poetic justice. The army found the toughest place in Germany to send me just to see if I could hack it.

Units at the rock go to the field a lot. Some spend six or more months per year training in the woods or the mud. The battalion I was assigned to went to the field on average about four months per year. I learned there aren't many enjoyable moments in the field. It is often wet and cold, and forces a person to be extremely creative in finding ways to make himself or herself comfortable. For example, it's amazing how many things can be done with a simple rain poncho. It can become a veritable house when you're out in the bush with nothing else. The only time the Rock looked good, and then the place seemed like paradise, is when I came out of the field. Three hots and a cot was never so good.

My unit was the 4th Battalion, 32nd Armored Regiment, of the 3rd Armored Division; nicknamed the Red Lions. Our uncompromising motto was "Victory or Death." We were a tank unit. As time passed I found this particular tank unit had a pretty good reputation. In 1988 our Abrams tanks shot the highest score ever recorded for a unit at gunnery training. We had the most advanced tanks and equipment in the army: the M1A1 Abrams tank; the Bradley fighting vehicle; and a bunch of those funny looking new jeeps called humvees. I guess when you put it all together, the equipment and our performance in training, we were, at that time, the best tank unit in the army. Probably the best tank unit in any army.

Our mission was to protect a huge pass in western Germany called the Fulda Gap. The Fulda Gap had been the chosen invasion route into that part of western Europe all through ancient and modern history. If the Russians were to attack West Germany they would surely come through the Fulda Gap. But, with 12,000 nuclear warheads in the U.S. arsenal pointed in their direction, most of us knew the Russians were never going to attack West Germany. I began to see our mission, then, as playing out some kind of historical balance. That balance of power had to exist, and we were it. Anyway, we all played our roles to the best of our abilities every day. We were being all we could be. Pretty soon I started thinking the Rock wasn't all that bad an assignment. Sure we went to the field, but only three or four months a year. That left eight or nine months back in garrison and all I needed was a pass or some leave and I could travel anywhere in Europe. Not Bad.

The Players

Everybody in the army has got a story. "Why the hell are you in the army?" is the most frequently asked question of any soldier. Everybody had some elaborate answer to why it is they did something so stupid as saying yes to Uncle Sam. Not that being in the army is the dumbest thing a person can do. It's just that after someone's been in uniform a while he or she gets the feeling that some justification is needed for putting themselves through hell.

Staff Sergeant Chris Thompson, better known as Sergeant T,

was my leader and mentor so to speak. I'd had leaders in the army who I either loved or hated, with most getting my respect. With Sergeant T, it was all three.

Sergeant T came from a tough working class neighborhood in LaCrosse, Wisconsin. There were many long hours around the camp stove in the field that he'd tell me about growing up in that tough neighborhood, the street fights and beer parties during his biker days, and just why the hell it was that he was in the army. We both came from the same neck of the woods in the upper Midwest. Though my background wasn't the tough biker type, I still understood him pretty well. We got along damn great, with an occasional hell of an argument. Most of the time I'd start the argument as there were things about the army that sure as hell made no sense to me. Every time I'd be raising hell about some ridiculous thing battalion was making us do I'd get this knowing look in his eye and then the slight crack of a smile. He'd stare at me with huge gray owl-eyes which were magnified by thick Coke bottle type glasses. "Do it anyway goddamnit," was the most likely reply.

After working with Sergeant T for some time I began to respect the knowledge he had in his job and his confident attitude in any situation. Sergeant T was a big man and inspired confidence in the soldiers he led. He did this in a way I've had a hard time understanding. He wasn't always a nice guy and he wasn't always fair. He could be real calm one minute and the next be yelling and screaming about some stupid thing someone had done. Sometimes this seemed a little unstable to me and I thought maybe it was due to a couple too many beer bottles over the head back in his biker days .... Though Sergeant T never graduated from high school he did have his GED. A street smart sharpness and his no bullshit candor inspired my confidence. I'd follow the son of a bitch to hell if that's where we had to go. I told him that, in

17

so many words, over a couple of beers during a back yard barbecue, after we'd pretty much been through hell anyway. I caught him staring at me pretty hard. "Funny," he said, "I had a master sergeant I told that same thing to once."

Sergeant T and I thought a lot alike.

The CO

The company commander (CO) for the majority of my tour with the Red Lion battalion was Captain Hanks. He was a small statured man with a quick wit and an equally quick ability to change his temperament. The CO for Headquarters company of the Red Lions had 300 men under his command. A CO is a dad to his troops sometimes and maybe that best describes Captain Hanks. Having so many troops to command takes a toll on a CO. It seems he was always dealing with family problems like marriage breakups, or young soldiers getting drunk and tearing up the barracks. Captain Hanks was the guy ultimately responsible for everybody in the company. The CO liked to let us think the pressure of his job drove him a little crazy, and maybe it did. This probably accounted for the occasional wild swings in his behavior. A person never did quite know how to take the CO and that suited him just fine. One day we were the best damn bunch of guys a CO could ever command and the next "a bunch of fuckin' idiots."

Captain Hanks was most famous for his friday afternoon safety briefing. It's army policy to have a safety briefing before a weekend. The CO had this down to an art. Invariably it was the same message every friday but it was always an event to see just what the CO would put emphasis on in any particular week. The basic points were: swim only in authorized areas; wear safety equipment when operating a lawn mower; don't get drunk and tear up 'his' billets; use a condom; and don't

18

be fucking another man's wife .... The CO would always end his friday briefing by telling us to look out for each other. He'd point out that for some of us the rest of the guys were the only family we had there. I guess we were his kids. Big Daddy Hanks. Sometimes it was Doc Hanks. He was also known as the Lone Wolf. His radio call sign; Lone Wolf 6. Lone Wolf for Headquarters Company, Hanks; 6 for commander.

Chapter 4
CAT's Meow

The man in charge of the Red Lion battalion when I first arrived was Lieutenant Colonel Stokes. Colonel Stokes had been in charge of the unit for some time and under him had gained its reputation as the best shooting tank battalion in the army. Under Colonel Stokes the Red Lions shot the first ever perfect scores in a downrange gunnery. To shoot a perfect score in a tank gunnery is some feat. One tank has to put 20 to 30 rounds downrange, with a time limit, at targets anywhere from 1000 to 3000 meters away, and never miss. It's even more impressive considering 3000 meters is about two miles. With the right crew an M1A1 Abrams tank, with its ability to determine range and then compute the firing elevation and direction of its 120 mm main gun virtually in an instant, is sophisticated to the point of almost never missing. In 1988 we proved that. Because we were such a good bunch of shooters, the brass at headquarters, US Army Europe, decided to enter us in a little friendly competition against the best tank gunners in all the rest of the NATO countries. The name of the competition was CAT; short for Canadian Army Trophy. The Canadians had started the competition a few years earlier and it happened every two years. In 1989 the US Army fielded two separate teams for the competition and one of them was a company from the mighty Red Lions.

There were four tank companies in the Red Lions and only one company could enter the competition. It would be Charlie company. It made sense that Charlie got the nod. They had the company with the two tanks that received those first ever perfect scores. The rest of us soon found out this CAT thing had a big reputation in the army. In 1987 the US had won the competition and the generals were gonna make damn sure we'd win it again. No expense was spared. The CAT team was issued fancy flight suit uniforms called Nomex; just like the ones jet pilots wear. They had them tailored to fit with colorful patches sewn on; even had their own patch made with a big Red Lion in the middle. The rest of us weren't authorized to wear Nomex so we had to wear our same old jungle fatigues, without colorful patches. When the CAT team went to the field to train, and they did this almost constantly for a year, they got the best meals; steaks, seafood. They even had their own sports psychologist! His job was to make sure they were in the right frame of mind before the competition, just like before a big game.

All these people getting the royal treatment made the rest of us feel just a little left out. It wasn't long before "CAT" team members were walking into places like the chow hall and hearing a chorus of meows. It wasn't that we were jealous, it was just the uniforms they got to wear. The people on the CAT team worked hard, I'll give them that. They went to the field all the time and I'm sure it caused a divorce or two. There was a lot of pressure on the CAT team to win this thing, but the rest of us felt we were playing second fiddle. Hard feelings were starting to show up between the CAT team and guys in the rest of the companies. It was petty when I look back on it, but words were being said back and forth nonetheless.

Finally the day of the competition came. There were seven or eight countries participating; US, Canada, Great Britain, France, West Germany, Belgium, and some long haired guys from the Netherlands. The Red Lion CAT team was reported to be in great shape. The sports psychologist the generals had hired to give our boys the edge made the decision to put our guys in isolation for 24 hours before the competition. The idea was to keep them focused on blowing holes in targets. All the other teams were in the cantina the night before the competition toasting to each other's health. The story was that the long haired guys

21

from the Netherlands were the biggest toasters. Partying the night before must be the key to a calm trigger finger because the guys from the Netherlands shot an almost perfect score and won the competition. Being isolated and thinking about nothing else for 24 hours would make anybody jittery. Our Red Lions finished second to last.

We were told Colonel Stokes had a regular assignment rotation, as he left the battalion one month after CAT. I remember thinking it was funny the Colonel would leave so quickly. We knew the generals had spent a number of millions of dollars on this competition and losing is bad for careers. That motto "Victory or Death" kept creeping into my brain whenever I thought about our old commander.

Colonel Cramer

So, we had a new battalion commander, Lieutenant Colonel Thomas Cramer, and boy were things about to change in the Red Lions. Everyone knew something was up when in his first speech to the battalion he explained that our main mission was to "Kill Fuckin' Russians!" Well, we all knew that our mission was to protect western Europe from a Soviet invasion, it's just that we were a peacetime army. I think the Colonel thought we were a little lax; peacetime and all. I suppose, though, when a person got right down to it, that was our mission; kill fuckin' Russians. Why hide the true nature of our day to day job. It wasn't long before the chaplain had gotten hold of Colonel Cramer. Some of the wives were in the theater the day and his speech hadn't gone over well with them. "Christ! Didn't those women know we had a war to fight!" was his reply, exaggerated somewhat as it made its way through the battalion. Sadly, Colonel "George Patton" Cramer, was less exuberant in his speeches after that.

Colonel Cramer was a thin wiry guy who pretty much kept

himself isolated at battalion HQ. Whereas Colonel Stokes' style was to know every person he commanded, I don't think Colonel Cramer ever knew my name or face during the two plus years I was in his command. That suited me just fine. The basic idea in army life is to keep a low profile. If people don't know you exist they don't come looking for you when a weekend detail pops up. In his mind, I believe he thought us commo support guys were not worthy. The Colonel was a tank commander, ready for battle. How could he take the time to speak to lowly commo pukes. His aloofness created problems for the battalion and the changes he was making were turning us upside down. Even though our radio down time was one of the lowest in the division, Colonel Cramer thought that commo needed fixing. He did this by taking away our platoon status, making us part of the overall maintenance platoon, mechanics and the like. That was alright, the mechanics were good guys. We had just lost our independence, that's all. Platoon Sergeant T was no longer a platoon sergeant and this did not make him happy. "It's all fucked up," the Colonels favorite saying, sums up what we were in for in the coming months.

Gunnery

"Just how the hell is it that in one year you can go from the best goddamn shootin' battalion in the army to the worst!? Over."

"Well sir, the battalion has been going through some changes and ...."

"I just can't believe these goddamn numbers. Half your tanks qualified. What the hell kind of shit is this, Tom? Over."

"Well sir, we're gonna go back and train just as hard as we can ...."

"Yeah, you're goddamn right that's what you're gonna do and

you're gonna make damn sure that when you come back to this sonofa-bitch next fall you qualify all those fuckin' tanks! Ready six, out."

"Hey Sergeant T, that's over an open net."

"You're goddamn right it is. He's tearing Colonel Cramer a new asshole ain't he?"

"It's hard to believe Colonel Nash would be tearing up Colonel Cramer that bad over an unsecured frequency."

"Yeah, for the whole world to hear. I think it's great! Serves the bastard right."

"Maybe there'll be some changes now," I said. "I mean we sure couldn't be doing much worse. Maybe some of the smart bastards will get the point and try not to change something that's worked pretty damn well."

"You know my motto, If it ain't broke don't fix it. I been trying to pound that into their thick fuckin' skulls for six, hell, eight months now. Hard to say if things will change, hard to say."

Sergeant T and I were listening to the radios that day at gunnery. It was April, 1990, at a place called Grafenwoehr, West Germany. Grafenwoehr was a huge tank and artillery training area cut out of the forests of northern Bavaria. Hitler had used this same area for training and after the war we took it over. The Red Lions had just had the worst gunnery performance in their history; maybe army history. Colonel William "Wild Bill" Nash, commander of the 1st Brigade, 3rd Armored Division, of which the Red Lion battalion was a part, had just given Lt. Colonel Cramer an ass chewing like I'd never heard. A rumble had developed between Sergeant T and battalion HQ over the changed support structure in the battalion and had been intensifying for months. The ass chewing tickled him to no end. It seemed to justify what he'd been talking about. The battalion was in an uproar and our performance at gunnery proved it.

The rumors started to fly about Colonel Cramer getting relieved of his command. This would have made Sergeant T, myself, and quite a few other people extremely happy. Since Colonel Cramer had taken over eight months previously things had gone from bad to worse. Getting used to the new system was taking an extremely long time. Add to this, the lingering effects of CAT were still with the battalion. The whole competition had driven a wedge between the soldiers of the Red Lions. For over a year it was CAT team this and CAT team that, while the rest of the battalion suffered greatly. Normal rotation to gunnery is every six months and we hadn't been to a full battalion gunnery for a year and a half. This delay was directly linked to CAT since training money was diverted to them at the expense of two full battalion gunneries. There were a lot of hard feelings toward CAT and company commanders were telling us we had to put it behind us. If the CAT team had won it probably would've been a little easier for the rest of the battalion to swallow. Instead, they'd gotten their asses kicked and that was hard on the whole battalion, especially the guys in Charlie company. We knew we had to get the battalion back up to speed. What we didn't know was just how quickly we'd need to do it.

Chapter 5
PLDC

It was that same spring of 1990 when Sergeant T decided that I should go to the promotion board and the infamous PLDC (Primary Leadership Development Course). The purpose being to make the rank of sergeant. I felt the advancement would be good as I knew that a little more rank would get me away from certain undesirable jobs that lower enlisted folks do on a regular basis. The word latrine comes to mind a lot here. My present rank was specialist E-4. Even though the rank is not called private, in reality we were just privates that were a little better paid. The insignia of the specialist rank has an eagle in the middle so we called the rank full bird private, like a full bird colonel.

First thing I had to do was pass a promotion board made up of all the company first sergeants and the battalion sergeant major. The board was no easy task. I would be put on the spot for 40 minutes to an hour and asked innumerable questions concerning everything from military customs and courtesies, to basic things about army life and current affairs. I had about a month to get ready for this board and Sergeant Milano, another NCO in my commo platoon (now the maintenance platoon), was my sponsor and teacher. Sergeant Milano was a multi-talented man who held a black belt in karate, wrote short stories, and talked a lot about being well endowed in the manhood area. He said it had something to do with his being Italian. Sergeant Milano had not a bone of humility in his body. One of his claims, and something he let everyone know, was that he was an excellent player of sports, basketball in particular. I won't take anything away from him. He was short statured but was a hell of a ball player and quick as a cat (his own words). He was also a running monologue of sports fact and trivia. It was his main, incessant, topic of conversation. In the field he listened to the radio in the mornings and then ran down the scores for everybody in the tent to hear. After that there would typically be a half hour monologue on how the three home runs that won the 4th game of the 1929 World Series affected the future course of baseball. Anyway, Sergeant Milano was a hell of a good talker, and so, was a good teacher. He figured those current affairs questions I would get at the board would be about sports, so I had numerous lectures on sports trivia.

Sergeant Milano and I trained steadily for the big day. In army life a promotion board is a big event and can cause a little anxiety. I had the usual nervousness, but hey, I'd gone to college. If I couldn't dazzle them with my incredible grasp of military knowledge, well then I'd have to dazzle them with my brilliance. If that didn't work there was always a last resort. The Red Lion code; if you can't dazzle them with brilliance, dazzle them with bullshit.

My confident attitude going into this thing overlooked one obstacle. That obstacle's name was Sergeant Major Cole. Even though the command sergeant major is the highest ranking NCO in a battalion, Sergeant Major Cole didn't generate a lot of respect. He was a big man. Very big. There is a weight and physical fitness standard in the army that every soldier, regardless of rank, must meet. Somehow Sergeant Major Cole met this standard year after year, but how he did it nobody knew. He had never been seen taking a physical fitness test. This test came around twice a year and the Sergeant Major always managed to be on leave when that test came around .... Actually, it wasn't my job to watch who took the PT test and who didn't. He was said to be obnoxious to people who came in front of his board. I figured he was probably obnoxious to the guys who talked about him being on leave when the PT test came around. The PT test and his weight were his own business. I was sure I'd do just fine in his board.

The big day came and I went to the board with Sergeant Milano at my side. The Sergeant Major said my uniform looked good. I did a few facing movements as instructed and sat down to be grilled for 45 minutes. As far as I could tell everything went pretty well. I was relaxed and got along fine with the five company first sergeants on the board. I had my military knowledge down and so I didn't have to use many of those dazzling techniques. It was just like having a conversation with the first sergeants; real comfortable. As Sergeant Milano and I left the board he started to laugh. I asked him what the hell was so funny and he said the whole time I was in there I was gesturing with my hands, and rarely did I address the first sergeants before I gave them my answer to their questions. I told him I could see no reason not to gesture with my hands, and maybe I did forget to address the first sergeants a few times, (military courtesy demands an address of rank before speaking to anyone of higher rank). Sergeant Milano thought that was hilarious.

I guess he had a right to laugh. I failed miserably. That afternoon I was in the Sergeant Major's office, along with the other Red Lions who had failed:

"Son, you acted like you were back on the block in there."

"Yes, Sergeant Major."

"You had the military knowledge stuff down, but this gesturing with your hands; it's good to be relaxed, but it's a respect thing. We're not just shootin' the bull at the local coffee shop."

"Yes, Sergeant Major."

"Now listen. I want all of you to come back here and give this thing another shot. Sometimes we've got to get knocked down and then fight our way back. That's what it takes sometimes to find out who we really are. That's how we build character. Y'all understand that?"

"Yes, Sergeant Major."

"Sometimes we've got to drag ourselves up! Overcome the odds. Bite down a little harder. Study a little more. That's when you've got to reach down inside yourself, "waaaay down inside," and pull out that last particle of strength that says I can do it! I can be a sergeant in the United States Army! When y'all come back in front of my board that's what I want you to tell me. Y'all understand that?"

"Yes, Sergeant Major!"

"I had one young man who came in front of my board and the first thing he did was knock on the door of the boardroom so hard the pictures fell off the wall behind me!! I looked at all the other first sergeants and said, 'Now this young soldier wants to be a sergeant in the United States Army!!' He came in and looked sharp. We asked him just a few questions and then gave him a perfect score. Can y'all understand what it is I'm looking for!?"

"Yes, Sergeant Major!!"

"Now I want you all to go back and study harder for this thing and then I want to see you in that boardroom next month! Y'all understand that!!?"

"Yes, Sergeant Major!!"

I don't care what anyone else said about the Sergeant Major. The fact of the matter is the man could give one hell of a speech. I don't know about the rest of the guys who heard his speech that day, but when I left his office I was motivated! I was ready to be a sergeant in the United States Army and if I had to knock down doors to get it, no problem! So that's what I did. I went in front of the same board the next month and did I pound like hell on the boardroom door. I guess that was the key because I got the green light and passed the board. I was now Specialist (P) Jones; the P for PROMOTABLE. Maybe it was the Sergeant Major's speech, but it wasn't long before guys in my platoon were calling me "Super P." We had an artist in the platoon name Diego Cook. Kid was great at caricature. He'd drawn just about everybody in the battalion at one time or another and mine was a cape with a big "P" on my chest. Yeah, I was motivated, and I told the guys that when I was "in charge" of them on the latrine cleanups .... I figure a guy to to start somewhere.

"You call that a shine on those boots, Sergeant?"

"Ahh, no, Sergeant."

"What excuse can you give me for the shape of those boots, Sergeant?"

"I have no excuse, Sergeant."

"No excuse!? You mean to tell me there is no reason you can give for the way those boots look, Sergeant?"

"Ahh, no, Sergeant. I mean, yes, Sergeant. I mean, there's no excuse, Sergeant."

"What's your name, Sergeant?"

I'd been in this school, or academy is what it was called, for less than one day and already this guy was writing me up. I thought the boots looked pretty good. I found out later they had to look like glass. In the coming days I would literally be able to see myself in the shine on a black combat boot. This was PLDC, and if I'd experienced hell previously in the army, the 3rd Armored Division NCO Academy would bring it to a new level. I can't say everything was bad about PLDC. My instructors and the training were top notch. I learned not only things that are military, but things about life too. Maybe only how to stay alive, but life never the less. My main impression of that school was spit and polish, an NCO named Roy Summerall, and my feet. In the third week they were hamburger.

30

They didn't call the place an academy for nothing. Part of being in an academy setting is the head game. Everywhere we walked on academy grounds we had to make square corners. I suppose places like West Point were the same way. I wondered what four years of making square corners would do to a person. When we went to chow we had to get our plate, do a square facing movement to get our food, then make a right face to get dessert. Taking a left face after dessert, we walked to our table, about faced to get our drinks, came back to the table, sat down with perfect posture, and ate in complete silence. And then there was sleep. We got very little; about three or four hours per night. The academy was spotless and it kept us up a good part of the night just to keep it that way. And the uniforms; they had to be pressed everyday and ironing takes up time. Spit shining boots to glass takes hours. Our wall lockers, too. Every spare uniform had to be pressed; buttons buttoned, zippers zipped, and dress right dress; just like we would wear it, and the instructors checked these little details often. Four and sometimes five formations would be held per day and we would not miss or be late to any one ever. One missed formation and goodbye academy; no exceptions. Perfect attention to detail. Perfect, perfect, perfect.

From the cleanliness of the showers to the press of our jungle BDU's (Battle Dress Uniforms), the standards on all levels at the academy were extreme. To understand it I had to put it in the perspective of, say, being stationed on a missile site with those short range nukes they had in Germany in the late 80's and early 90's. The standard there must be perfection. One fuck up, "Boom." It's World War III.

Everyone was assigned to a 14 member squad and each squad had two instructors. Ours were Sergeant Summerall and Sergeant Cross. Sergeant Summerall was pretty easy going, Sergeant Cross just the opposite. It was the good cop, bad cop thing. I'd had the same experience in boot camp. One drill sergeant was a pretty good guy, you could come to him if you had a problem. The other scared the shit out of me. Sergeant Cross was the bad cop, and he was big enough to strike fear deep in the heart of any man.

About two weeks into the school I found out Sergeant Summerall was with the Red Lions before he had come to the academy. He still wore our "Victory or Death" unit crest on his dress uniform. He talked about going back to our combat unit after he was done teaching at the school. Sergeant Summerall was a master tank gunner with my battalion and talked to us a lot about being a tanker. He had a tall, rough hewn appearance, with dark, intelligent features, deep set eyes, and a trimmed, black mustache above his lip. He told us he was 29 years old and I was surprised because he looked and acted older. Teachers at the academy were all outstanding in one way or another. Being an instructor there was a good assignment for an NCO and looked pretty good in a 201 personnel file when promotion time came around. The army didn't let just anybody become an instructor at the academy. In Sergeant Summerall's case he had become one of the youngest master tank gunners in the army. He received that title as an E-5 buck sergeant; the first ever at that rank. Becoming a master gunner is an extreme test and only a few hold the honor. Sergeant Summerall was the best at what he did and was not shy in letting us know that fact.

One of the main themes the academy taught us as prospective NCO's, believe it or not, was compassion. The army is made up of many young soldiers who often are away from home for the first time. In teaching us to be leaders of young soldiers, compassion for personal problems associated with army life was stressed often. One particular day a suicide that had happened the year before was brought up in class. A student had gone up to the fourth floor of the academy and jumped out a window. The stress of the school was brought up and the topic of suicide prevention was discussed. Sergeant Summerall chose this time to talk about personal events in his own life.

He had been divorced the year before and he told us about his children and their mother. There was a custody battle over the children and he talked about how little he'd seen of them recently. Army life is hard on families. Field time and other duties keep them separated many months of the year. Sergeant Summerall talked about how much he loved his kids and how he missed seeing them. He showed us their pictures often. Even though he was hard on the outside, when he let his guard down there was something decent underneath. He taught us about values and in doing so expressed his own. He believed deeply in traditional things like loyalty and courage. I wondered if those traditional values got him in trouble in this changing world. Like a man who had learned chivalry in an age with no chivalry, he seemed lost somehow that day; a man with a hard kind of grace in a graceless age. He told us that the divorce had led him to excessive drinking and thoughts of his own mortality. I think Sergeant Summerall had a purpose in telling us about his failings and problems. That day we all felt great compassion for this man. Had he used his own problems to teach us about compassion? Or was it just the expression of a shattered ideal? I don't know ....

After 28 days of road marches; during land navigation in the 3rd week we were marching 10 to 15 miles a day and I did it in new boots (I made sure my boots looked good, even though my feet were ground chuck at the end of it); 12 hour days in the classroom, and other small tortures, I graduated from the academy. It was June of 1990 and about two weeks after graduation I ran into Sergeant Summerall at my barracks on the Rock. He said he was done teaching at the academy and was assigned back to the Red Lions in command of a tank crew. I had a strange feeling seeing Sergeant Summerall on the Rock that day. I couldn't quite place it, but maybe it had to do with the odd coincidence that my instructor at the academy happened to be directly from my unit, and then reassigned to it right after I'd met and got to know him. There were only two NCO academy's in Europe at the time, so this school took in soldiers from all over northern Europe. Innumerable units sent candidates to that school, units with at least 100,000 soldiers all combined.

I remember that moment and feeling, instinctively, that this "coincidence" was more than just that. Of course there is more to the story of my days at the academy and Sergeant Summerall. During the last week of academy training we all got into our dress uniforms and had a dinner. It was an initiation of sorts with a drinking of the "grog" (a mixture of many different alcoholic beverages and God knows what else), and skits by different platoons at the academy. Sergeant Summerall came to this event drunk as a skunk. Of course the first sergeants and the sergeant major were there and he made quite an impression. We were allowed to write a critique of the course at graduation, telling what we would like changed and our impressions. I wote about Sergeant Summerall in that critique, figuring he was in trouble at the academy, and trying to tell in my own words the kind of person I thought he was. It seems that critique forged something unspoken between us.

So, seeing Sergeant Summerall on the Rock that day, I somehow knew there was something in store for us. I could feel the future, as yet unseen. If we can, at times, glimpse into something that is so much greater than just ourselves, then at that instant, I was peeking into it. I can give no other explanation for my almost "deja vu" like feeling at that moment. Hindsight has shown that my impressions were quite real.

I saw Sergeant Summerall around the battalion quite a bit from then on. He'd come down to the commo shop occasionally and we'd pass the time talking about PLDC days. I had a deep respect for the man. He'd recently been "God" in my life for 28 days and I suppose this added to that respect heartily. Maybe I was beginning to idolize him. I know there were guys in his tank crew who were. He was merely one of the best tank gunners in the army. Chances are he was the best, the best that ever was. I don't know. In the coming months he'd have his chance to prove it.

Chapter 6
Training

It was the last week of July 1990. We were on a field training exercise in a place called Wildflecken, West Germany. Wildflecken was set in the rolling forests and valleys on the East-West German border, a border that would soon cease to exist. It was dirty and dusty there in July, and cold. Even in July Germany can be cold.

During this particular field exercise we trained a great deal for chemical and biological warfare. Wearing a gas mask and putting on all the gear associated with a chemical warfare environment is no fun. The M-17 gas mask is a molded piece of rubber that clamped onto my face like a vise. If I were claustrophobic I couldn't have stood the thing for more than a few seconds. The filter system constricts air flow so I had to practice deep controlled breathing. The gas mask I had was too small for my face. I guess I thought small was better because if the thing was tight, well, than nothing that wasn't suppose to get in would get in, right? The problem with my logic was painfully obvious after only a few minutes. The top of my forehead started aching; a kind of numbness that spread to my whole face and head, making the pain the only thing I could think about.

In my army career, training for survival in a chemical environment had been stressed constantly. This particular field training at Wildflecken was different, though. The battalion had set up an elaborate test site where each task associated with surviving a chemical war was stressed individually. I'd been in the army, all together, about three years at that point and had never seen such intense training on one particular subject.

The chemical equipment individual soldiers use is called MOPP gear. In army jargon that's Mission Oriented Protective Posture. There are five levels to MOPP. Mopp 0 is the gas mask strapped to a soldiers side in its carrying case. A charcoal suit, boots and gloves, which comprise the rest of the posture, within reach. MOPP 1 is the charcoal suitpants and top put on over regular clothes. MOPP 2 is like MOPP 1, but with rubber boots put on over regular combat boots. MOPP 3 is like MOPP 2, but with the gas mask donned and cleared on a soldiers face. At MOPP 4, in addition to all these other steps, a pair of long rubber gloves are worn. When I was at MOPP level 4 I was completely protected to army standard, and no matter how cold it was outside I was sweating like crazy. The charcoal suit must be the warmest garment of any army issue clothing; warmer than the parka I was issued. It's great when it's cold, murder when it's hot. At Wildflecken we trained relentlessly in the five MOPP levels.

Most of us despised the extra training. In my entire army career I must have put on the gas mask thousands of times. Army standard for getting a mask out of its case, donned and cleared on a soldiers face, is nine seconds. I had no problem meeting that standard. I was an expert. We were all experts. I could recite the five MOPP levels forward, backward, upside down and in my sleep; yet we trained on.

There are certain things in the army we were allowed to bitch about. Number one was chow. It is the God given right and duty of anyone in uniform to bitch about army chow. Second is guard duty. There's a hell of a lot of it. It's a fact of army life I had to live with. Third is the repetitive training. Army training is practice through repetition. From boot camp on, the tasks I had to learn were drilled into my head over and over and over. Things like weapons maintenance, map reading, first aid, and chemical warfare training all became the routine tasks we trained on day in and day out. Getting right down to it, that was our only mission in peacetime. Train. Over and over and over. News reporters said we were the best trained army in history. That was no bull.

We were getting an occasional Stars and Stripes newspaper while we were there. The Stars and Stripes caters to overseas military personnel all over the globe. We also listened frequently to Armed Forces Radio broadcasts from Frankfurt. Saddam Hussein was massing troops on the border of Kuwait. A lot of guys were asking Saddam who?, and Kuwait? Most of us knew, though, who the guy was. He was in the news a lot with the gassing of his own people, the Kurds, who had rebelled against his dictatorship in Iraq. Chemical weapons plants and the possibility he had nuclear arms was talked about all the time, and we got a lot of this news. I remember thinking this was the reason for all the chemical training. Did I imagine that some far-sighted individuals in my battalion, and possibly all the way up the chain of command to the Pentagon, had, in July of 1990, before Saddam invaded Kuwait, knew something the rest of us didn't? .... Naaa.

Two days after we finished training at Wildflecken, Saddam Hussein invaded Kuwait. Six days later, on 8 August, the first American troops were sent to Saudi Arabia. Everyone in the Red Lion battalion watched the events in the desert with great interest. When the first troops were sent into the region, most of us, myself included, felt things would have to get really out of hand before troops from Germany were sent. I remember Sergeant T saying that units had never been pulled from Germany for a war someplace else. We still had a real world job, didn't we? Deter Russian aggression. Of course the Berlin wall had fallen in November of the previous year and talk of the Cold War was almost non-existent. Still, we'd been in Germany a long time. Desert warfare was totally opposite the type of thing we trained for. Most of us thought we'd be the last troops ever sent to the desert.

We went about our day-to-day routine. As the weeks passed the number of troops and units President Bush was sending to the Gulf increased dramatically. In September news reports said two and three hundred thousand. That was a lot of troops and some of us started thinking maybe German-based U.S. troops would be sent. Some small units like the 12th Aviation brigade out of Frankfurt had gone, but there was no word about major troop call ups from Europe. About mid-September, though, it seriously crossed my mind that maybe something was up.

Fall Gunnery

About this time we loaded up and moved out to Grafenwoehr for fall gunnery training. This was the place where just a few months before the Red Lions had experienced the worst gunnery performance in its history.

Gunnery isn't real hard field time. Usually our unit was assigned barracks with the PX exchange, laundromat, and movie theater located close by. During the evenings we could catch a movie, then have a couple beers or play some cards at the Red Lion lounge; a place the battalion set up for relaxation at gunnery (I think CAT proved the value of being relaxed at a tank gunnery). Anyway, all in all, it was pretty cushy. For this gunnery, though, the Red Lions were assigned to tents. The PX, laundromat and movie theater were miles away. I figure the units who do the best at gunnery always get the best barracks, the ones closest to those main facilities. At the previous two gunneries the Red Lions were assigned barracks right across the street from those main facilities. That's when we were the best shooters in the army. Oh, how quickly they forget.

We set out to again prove that we were the best. In commo an intensive maintenance schedule was set up to service every radio in the battalion before and during gunnery. If the tankers didn't hit targets it wasn't going to be because they weren't talking to each other, or to the guys in the towers controlling the courses.

It's always a lot of work for commo guys at gunnery. We had separate radios we'd install in every tank before it went downrange. With that radio the guys in the range command tower could hear all intercom conversation inside the tank as the crew went through the routine of seeing targets and firing rounds. There are four crewmen in an M1A1 Abrams tank. Driver, gunner, loader, and commander. When the gunner sights a target he yells through the intercom system the type of cannon round needed to kill the target. He has two choices. The 120 mm sabot round, an armor piercing thin arrow type projectile used for distance and sheer killing power, and the 120mm heat round, a phosphorous type projectile used to burn through smaller targets exploding and melting everything inside. The commander will yell "SABOT!", telling the loader to draw that round from his storage area in the rear of the turret. Once the round is loaded "UP!" is yelled by the loader, the gunner then pulls the triggers yelling "ON THE WAY!". The sabot round leaves the muzzle of the 120 mm main gun at a velocity of 1,650 meters per second, about one mile per second, or approximately Mach 4. Total time to target sighting and round flying downrange should be under 5 seconds and this is why the range tower controllers want to hear what's going on inside that tank.

To make this work we used a PRC-77 (Prick-77) radio (the same radio carried on the back of every Vietnam era radio man) with a modified cable containing a specific diode, connected directly to an intercom box inside the tank turret. The diode allowed the prick-77 to be "keyed" (set to a talk position) continuously on a separate tower "freq." (frequency), thereby letting the tower hear that intercom conversation. It's a pretty fancy setup and was a hell of a lot of work. In one of my first experiences at gunnery we ran two companies through two downrange runs each. I had to install, then recover the prick-77 at the end of the run, for each tank. With 14 tanks in a company and two companies, we had 28 tanks. I climbed in and out of each of these tanks four times. Once to put the radio in and once to take the radio out, for two separate runs. The gunneries go on all night so our shifts were a straight 24 hours. During that 24 hour period I'd climbed up into and down out of a tank 112 times.

There was a lot of activity at the Grafenwoehr ranges during this gunnery. It was here that I began to get the feeling we really were gearing up to fight a war. Artillery rounds were being fired 24 hours a day, sometimes right over the areas where we lived and worked. There's something about a whistling artillery shell flying overhead that didn't quite set right with me, though I couldn't quite put my finger on what made me feel that way ....

Getting used to the booming racket of a gunnery area was always tough, especially for the first few days. I'd go airborne at least a foot from my cot when at 2:00 a.m. a booming 155 mm howitzer fired its rounds close to camp. It amazed me, though, that after a week or so I'd fall to sleep and not hear the racket all night.

Master Gunner

About nine or ten days into gunnery I ran into Sergeant Summerall at the Charlie company maintenance truck. He was talking with Sergeant Hawkins, the Charlie company commo man. Sergeant Hawkins was another compadre in our defunct commo platoon. Since there were only six of us in commo we all stayed pretty tight. He was a big burly South Dakota farm boy. I thought of him as Hayseed, though never called him that. Seemed he should have been standing in a field, chaff of wheat hanging from his mouth, hands in the pockets of his Osh Kosh coveralls.

Of the 58 tanks in the Red Lions, Sergeant Summerall had just shot the highest score of any. Word went around quickly who had the best score. I was in no way surprised in hearing that news, so I stopped to congratulate him.

"I figured you'd be blowing things away out there, Sarge."

"Yeah, got a good crew. Real good kids." He looked over at Sergeant Hawkins, "I had this guy in PLDC and he never said anything in class." He often gave me a hard time for not saying much in his classes (I'd been in a sleep starved stupor most of the time).

"I always spoke up, Sarge, when I had something to say."

"That sure the hell wasn't very often." He paused. "You know I still think about that female we had in the class who didn't make it through map reading. What was her name?"

"Davis, yeah," I said. She'd been to PLDC once before and she'd failed map reading that time, too. "It was some kind of mental block for her when she took that test because she had that material down, Sarge." Davis had failed the first test we were given in the subject. The school gave us two chances to pass each test. I knew how to read a map, so Sergeant Summerall had me tutoring Davis to pass the second test, but she failed that one too. She'd never be allowed back into the school having failed twice.

"I thought she had the material down, too," he said. "It just wasn't that goddamn hard."

"Maybe I'm not a very good tutor."

"I was the damn teacher. You did alright."

42

"Can't win 'em all."

"Yeah, can't win 'em all."

During this gunnery we proved again our ability to shoot tank rounds downrange. Whereas six months earlier we had met army qualification standards on only half our tanks, this time it was 100%. The Red Lions of past years, the ones who seemed to never miss, were back.

We returned from gunnery at the end of September. By that time the rumors about going to the Gulf were flying. We watched as more and more units were called. Still, no German based U.S. divisions had been given orders for the desert.

It was the last week in October and I was watching CNN News, on the Armed Forces Television Network, in my barracks room. Secretary of Defense Dick Cheney was coming on to announce major new troop call ups for the Persian Gulf. Finally, about 8 o'clock German time, the Secretary came on the screen. He announced huge movements of German based U.S. troops. The 3rd Armored Division, of which the Red Lions were a part, would be sent on or about the first of the New Year.

A television news report is how myself and the rest of the Red Lions learned we were going to the desert. The army was as tuned into Cable News Network (CNN) as the rest of the world. Months later CNN would, at times, prove to be a more reliable source of information than our command. I remember seeing a comic depicting a room full of generals watching CNN for the latest intelligence on the war. There was some truth to that.

I remember some pretty mixed feelings when I heard the news. On the one hand we'd been expecting this announcement for some time. On the other, something like this is impossible to completely prepare for. A lot of bravado like, "It's about time," or "Call your mother cause her baby's going to war," reverberated through the barracks. It quickly died. As everybody hit the rack, disquieting silence filled the space.

Part II

Chapter 7
Tent City

After hearing, on the television news, that the division was going to the desert, we waited for word from our commanders. That came the next day and it made me feel no better. The Red Lions, as part of 3rd Armored Division, would depart Germany for the deserts of Southwest Asia on or about the first of the new year. At least it was official.

We had two months before deployment and there was a hell of a lot of work to do. To get our equipment ready for the trip we had to service all of it and repair where needed. We had to get our houses in order. Things like how the bills were going to be paid were suddenly a big thing. For guys with families it was making sure everyone was taken care of while they were gone. A lot of guys sent their families back to the States. Captain Hanks, in one of his famous speeches, told us to plan to be away one year. He said it was better to plan for the long haul, we wouldn't be disappointed if it happened we stayed that long. A year is a long time. I didn't think we'd be gone that long; at least I prayed like hell we wouldn't.

I called home and told the family I was going to the desert. I'd been preparing them some time for this possibility. During all my recent phone calls I'd said it was very possible we would eventually be called there, so when the news came I don't think it was such a big shock. I thought about my mother. I think in many ways it was a bigger hell for the people back home than it was for the men and women who were actually there. Families have to watch the news every night, being reminded they have a loved one in such a dangerous place. For the people who are there it's just living day to day. You don't have time to worry about what the hell will happen tomorrow. A person just does his or her job. I had a lot of confidence; in myself, and especially in those guys around me, those guys in the tanks. We knew we were the best there was. There was no other way to think.

I was born in 1960. One of the earliest things I remember is watching the television news almost every night about the war in Vietnam. When I was seven or eight years old that war was my perspective on how things were in the world. It had, after all, gone on my whole life. About that time I very clearly remember asking my mother when would I go to war? She told me that by the time I was old enough for such a thing, there may not be a war to fight. I remember listening to what she said with disbelief. "How could there not be a war?," I remember thinking. It seemed funny and unbelievable to me that there would not be a war going on all the time. It was the natural order of things. It was a constant that had existed since the beginning of my conscious memory. I figured for sure I'd have to fight in one some day. To the question I posed to my mother when I was eight years old, I now knew the answer. 1991.

Going, Going, Gone

"Can you guys give me a ride from Baghdad to Jordan?"

"I imagine we can squeeze you in, man. We've got a lot of equipment to haul. It'll be tight in there and it's a hell of a trip across that desert."

"I'll manage. You guys are with the press, ha."

"Yeah, we're here watching Saddam's latest moves in Kuwait."

"It's good to see some Americans. How long before you're pulling out? It seems I'm in a bit of a hurry." There were soldiers all over the damn place and that made me just slightly uneasy.

"We'll be pulling out in just a few minutes. Those soldiers

bother you, ha."

"You bet. Anytime you guys are ready."

I'd been posing as an aide to Saddam Hussein. For whom I was really working I didn't know, but it seemed I had a mission. I had managed to infiltrate Hussein's government and had somehow gained their trust. Last night I'd been assigned to guard Hussein while he slept. I remember thinking I could solve one hell of a lot of the world's problems by taking a gun to this man's head. All of a sudden the .38 is in my hands. It was simple. End his life and end a destructive war about to happen. I put four of those bullets into his head. "Bang, bang, bang, bang." Now I'm with these reporters in an old white sedan, flying across the desert. Jesus, I hope this car makes it. Are those troops around the palace following? I've got to figure a way across the border. They will know of the assassination by the time we get there .... Got to get the hell out of this country.

I awoke to darkness. Sleep edged toward consciousness. It was only a dream!, but so real. My God. It was an overwhelming relief when I thought he was dead. I wouldn't have to go to some desert and risk my life. It was so easy putting those bullets into his head. I didn't hesitate one moment pulling the trigger .... God help me.

It was New Year's Eve. First light would be in an hour or so. During the last two months we had serviced every piece of equipment in the battalion. Then it was packed and convoyed to the ports where it was loaded on great ships. We'd been poked and stuck with needles, given every possible vaccine known to man, medically checked, then rechecked. I'd been examined ten different times, it seemed, to see if there was anything physically wrong with me, something that would prevent me from going. There was nothing. I was lean, mean, and going to the desert.

It wasn't that I was eager to go. It's just that it seemed inevitable. I had become convinced there was some larger force driving these events. I was simply a part of them and nothing I could do would stop my participation in them. I am simply here to see, to observe them if you will. If I think about all of it that way it seems to be easier; like I can detach myself from it somehow because I feel I am only an observer. The detachment is only in my mind, for sure. The rest is completely realistic. It is really happening.

When I rolled out of my comfortable bunk in the barracks on that New Year's Eve morning in 1990, I knew it was the last comfortable mattress I would be on for some time. I tried to lie there a few extra minutes just to savor it. I got up that morning, took a slow, long hot shower, and knew it would be the last one of those for a while, too. There'd be little hot water for showers where I was going.

For two months I'd been packing. I'd bought all kinds of practical little things I'd need for this "excursion." One of the things I thought about a lot was how to stay clean. I was preparing for a one year stint. One year in a dirty, hot, sweaty environment; probably with little water at times. Hygiene is super important in such a place. A person could catch something out there and never get rid of it.

I bought about 500 of those wet-wipe things, they'd come in handy: extra toothpaste, soap, and toilet paper. I wear glasses, so the army ordered me four extra pair of the infamous BC glasses (BC for Birth Control). We called them birth control glasses because they were so damn ugly a guy would never get laid wearing them. Two pair were prescription sunglasses. I would definitely need them.

We'd gotten all our gear down to the gymnasium on the Rock that New Year's Eve day. We were waiting for buses that would take us to Rhein Main Air Base in Frankfurt. I had brought my camera, a little pocket 35 mm, and decided to record everything. I needed to get my hair cut and got one of my buddies, Green, to do it. Green was one of the born-again Christian types. He took a bit of a hard time around the battalion because guys thought he was trying to convert them. Truth is, some guys probably needed converting to the Lord about then. Green and I got along fine.

A bunch of those buddies stand out in my memory that day. Guys like Evans; a kid from Indiana, no older than 18. BoschCordonna; with that name I always asked him if he wasn't secretly a hit-man for the mob. Pacos; young, sharp Indian kid from Arizona, said he'd never been with a woman, was waiting till he got married. Garcia; a scout, always said I looked and acted exactly like his uncle. I told him his uncle must be a hell of a guy. Garcia would see a lot of action in that scout platoon. A lot of serious faces that day; crying wives and kids .... It was early evening when the buses came rolling in.

Rhein Main is a one hour ride from the Rock. We arrived there about 1900 hours that evening. We were taken to a huge German fest tent where the USO had set up a place we could relax. There was plenty of food, books we could take, movies to watch. It was the main stopover point for all troops headed to the Gulf from the States and Germany. There were all kinds of signs on the walls listing people's names with different stateside and German based U.S. units they were from. Our plane was to leave at 2200 hours, but we soon found out we would be delayed. We were told there was a generator problem on the plane, so I found a place on a big couch and tried to relax. Soon it was 2300 hours and we started to think about celebrating the new year; it was an afterthought. There didn't seem to be much to celebrate. There was none of the bubbly. From that moment on I realized we would be alcohol free; a stiff sentence for some of the guys I worked with.

Finally it was midnight and a less than enthusiastic yell went up from the GI's in the USO tent. We did have little cups of fruit punch to toast each other with, compliments of the nice ladies who manned the USO tent. There were two pretty German girls who came around with a bowl of one pfennig pieces. They are about the same value as a penny. It's good luck in Germany to take one and put it in your pocket on New Years Eve. I still have that pfennig.

We decided to get a picture with the two pretty German girls. It was the young kid Evans, another guy in the platoon named Martinez, and myself. We took the pictures in front of an incredibly large American flag that was set up in the USO tent. I felt like a true patriot, my arms around two pretty girls in front of a huge American flag on the day I was going off to fight the war. The best picture was of Martinez with a big cheese-eatin' grin on his face. Martinez was afraid that picture would get back to his very pretty wife. That bothered him a lot and he was always coming around asking about that picture. After he'd asked me for the tenth time I finally gave it to him. The two pretty girls hardly spoke English, but wore big smiles in the pictures we took. The last two pretty faces I would see for a long time.

About 0100 hours we were told that our flight would not leave until noon that day. We were directed to a supply tent and issued a pillow and blanket, then sent to one of the tents set up to house the transient troops. I found a cot. It had been a long day and I fell quickly off into a deep sleep.

It was more a feeling than an actual sight. I could feel the blackness and it was completely terrifying. It was an encompassing, surrounding blackness; a furious, smoky blackness. Even more than the blackness, though, was the sense of terror and destruction; massive, deadly destruction. The destruction is creating the billowing blackness! This I could feel. Deep, gut-wrenching terror, and sorrow;

sickening sorrow.

The dislocation of unfamiliar surroundings left me struggling to remember where I was. A sweaty, achiness surrounded me. The dream left me with the feeling of death; like I was mourning the loss of something, someone. At the end of the dream I felt a warning, a plea of some kind. The picture and feeling the dream created was terrifying and powerfully moving. The dream beckoned to me. It was telling me something.

As I crawled out of my cot that New Year's Day the dream was very fresh in my memory. I remember feeling an overwhelming compulsion to write someone. A reasonable solution had to be found for what was happening in the crazy part of the world I was heading to. To whom could I write? I decided to go right to the top. The commander-in-chief himself; George Bush. I threw on my jungle BDU's, pulled pen and notebook out of my pack, and went over to the USO tent for breakfast. There I drafted my letter to the President:

"....Being in the Army I am trained for war and will carry out my mission to the letter if war becomes our option .... I believe Hussein is looking for an out in this crisis. Anyone with an ounce of rationality, of which he must have some, would be looking for that."

Saddam Hussein, rational? Ha Ha. The letter went on to state a policy to avert war that makes little sense now. I never sent the letter. Maybe I thought the hour was too late already. The US, along with the UN, had given the deadline of 15 January for Hussein to leave Kuwait. Things were going to happen quickly from now on. No matter how many ways I looked at this situation, there was not an easy answer.

As I finished writing the letter that New Year's Day morning in the USO tent, a bunch of jarhead Marines had just arrived from a stateside unit and had gotten in the breakfast line. The Marines had the sharp looking desert BDU's, while all we had were the regular green jungle BDU's. We were supposed to get our desert uniforms when we arrived in the desert, we'd see about that. The breakfast wasn't much. There was some sausage and ham, and some Christmas cookies the volunteer ladies had brought in. I had two MRE's to eat anyway. The army's Meals Ready to Eat would do incredible things to my digestive system in the coming months.

Finally, after an hour or two, the news came over the PA system that we were to board our flight. I went back to the tent and grabbed my gear.

Our plane was an Eastern Airlines L-1011. I'd heard Eastern was bankrupt and when the plane had broken down I didn't feel all that comfortable getting on the thing. We got off the ground, though, and I felt better when we were in the air. It was a very good flight. We had pretty stewardesses waiting on us hand and foot. I remember seeing a stewardess crying in the rear galley, I didn't know what that was about. I heard some of the guys in my battalion had flown down in C-141 transport planes. The stories about them were not good. Getting a civilian charter flight was good luck.

The flight, with a refueling stop in Rome, lasted eight hours and I had a lot of time to think about where it was we were heading. I thought about Captain Hanks' speech as we were getting ready to leave. He was trying to prepare our brains for this thing. He looked at all of us and said it was his job to bring us all back, though he knew not all of us would. He said that when we get to the desert we had better be thinking straight with our shit together. If we were "FUCKIN STUPID" we wouldn't come back. The CO had a way with words. I looked at the rest of the guys sitting around me. They all seemed to be absorbed in their own thoughts. It was, I suppose, something I'll call "instant reality." It was a very quiet flight.

We landed in the desert at 2300 hours, 1 January, 1991. The place was King Faud Airport outside the city of Dhahran, Saudi Arabia. The plane simply stopped at the end of a desolate runway and we got off. When my feet hit the ground I took a big breath of air to test it out. It was very light. I thought the air might be devoid of some oxygen with no plants or trees to make it there. It was warm, about 60 degrees, and very dark. It was a half mile hike to a pickup point where some buses were to take us to Dhahran. We grabbed our gear and started walking.

The battalion maintenance officer was with us at the pick up point. Chief Wilson told us he'd been to the desert before in Egypt. He lectured us on staying clean. He said he still had something, a rash, that he hadn't gotten rid of from his first trip to the desert. He told us to drink six liters of bottled water per day. At the pickup point there was bottled water everywhere. Cases of the fancy Evian brand water littered the area. People were paying good money for that stuff back in the States. Here I'd be brushing my teeth and shaving with it every day. I thought that drinking six liters of water a day was extreme, and even during the hottest days when spring came I could never manage more than three. We grabbed our first bottles of Evian and started slugging it down.

Finally the buses came, the drivers being the first Arabs we saw. They had the traditional long white robes and kafka (Arab head-dress). The buses were regular city buses with dirt and dust from the desert caked on them inside and out. It didn't look like they'd ever been washed. On the trip to Dhahran I took notice of the new construction in and around the city. My impression was that a lot of money was being pumped into this place; big money. Newly built office buildings and housing under construction could be seen from the brand new super highway we were driving on. It was impressive, except for the buses, and the crazy bus drivers. They raced each other into the city that night, playing cat and mouse at 70 miles per hour. I wondered if I wouldn't be killed in a damn bus before I ever made it to the war.

We were dropped off next to the port area of Dhahran. Huge warehouses with thousands of cots laid out in rows housed U.S. troops. They had cement floors with a good roof. It didn't look too bad. There was even a housing area called the MGM Grand they were putting troops in. That sounded pretty good. Maybe we'd go there. By the time we were dropped off at this "Cement City" as it was called, first light was not far off. We'd been up some 24 hours at this point, but I wasn't greatly tired.

We waited around for word on where we were to stay. We ate a pretty good breakfast and at about 0800 hours buses came and we were told to get on. All our personal gear had met us here from the plane. I had two of the big green army duffel bags full of gear, and my rucksack. It all weighed well over 100 lbs. I dragged my gear to the buses and threw it on. We left Cement City and traveled in the early morning light along the coast of the Persian Gulf. The Gulf was spectacular in the mornings; a massive blue-green jewel sparkling in the morning sun. I watched seagulls glide over its smooth expanse; blue sky meeting waves at the horizon. Finally, after maneuvering through more than one checkpoint, we came upon a small peninsula, the Gulf waters surrounding it on the north and south. Large 25 man army green tents, in rows stretching one quarter mile long, and at least that deep, filled the small, sandy peninsula. It was the most army green tents I'd ever seen in one place, or imagined I'd ever see. "Tent City," Dhahran, Saudi Arabia; my home for the next 23 days.

Chapter 8
The King's Chefs

Tent City was big, three or four hundred tents with six to eight thousand troops. Living there those first few weeks in country gave us time to get to know our surroundings and get acclimated to the weather. Truth of the matter is, though, there was little acclimation needed. The weather was not very different from Germany; cold and wet. And our surroundings: Sierra, Alpha, November, Delta. SAND!

My first day at Tent City I worked to get situated with the rest of my platoon. Some had arrived earlier on other flights, so a tent had already been assigned to us. Sergeant T and Sergeant Milano were on those earlier flights and had carved out a niche for commo in a corner of the tent. The floors of the tents were sand, not the cement I had seen earlier in the day at the warehouse areas. No problem. The sooner I became used to sand the better.

We were living right in the port area of Dhahran and I watched the great ships come in and out every day. The battalion's equipment, except for a few command vehicles, hadn't arrived and we didn't expect it until after the 15th of January. Two guys from our platoon, Dog and Sergeant Smith, had been assigned to make the trip in the ships with our vehicles. Dog was known as the biggest womanizer and partier in the platoon. I don't know how he got the name Dog, it just seemed to fit. Sergeant Smith, on the other hand, was a tough, squared away E-5.

Sergeant Milano was in his usual form while we were in Tent City. He was still able to catch the basketball scores as we had an Armed Forces Network radio station which kept us informed on what was happening back in the States. Sergeant Milano and I speculated a lot about what was going to happen in the coming days. The UN had given Saddam the deadline of 15 January to get out of Kuwait and we both felt it would be in the man's best interest to pull out before the deadline. We were watching tanks roll off the ships 24 hours a day. In the parking areas next to the shipping docks a sea of M-1 tanks were lined up in perfect formation. These parking areas stretched for miles along the dock and were full of military hardware. Thousands of tanks, infantry fighting vehicles, armored personnel carriers, self-propelled howitzers, and trucks filled the lots. Granted, at that time Hussein did have the fourth largest army in the world which was something no one took lightly, including the tankers in the Red Lions. I remember a conversation with a tanker in Delta company about the 4000 tanks in Saddam's arsenal. The guy was visibly shook up when that number was mentioned. Still, why would Saddam bring down on his country the destruction all this firepower could bring?

About three days after I arrived at Tent City we were told that Iraqi U-boats had been seen in the Gulf just off our position and destroyed by US special forces units. Our commanders decided we'd better dig in. Digging in is what I remember most about desert life. Everywhere we went we dug in. The commanders lined tanks and Bradley's from other units along the sea wall that separated us from the Gulf and after about a half day's work we had some good positions dug out. Every tent had a chest level deep foxhole in the front and rear, large enough to accommodate every man in the tent.

Rumors?

Stories floated around all the time concerning this event or that. A person had a hard time knowing what to believe sometimes. I found it the best policy to take most things at face value. In other words, whether it was naive or not, I had to believe the stories were probably true:

The day we were digging foxholes some guys from the 1st Infantry Division, who were at Tent City with us, had dug about six feet down with a tunnel-like crevice off the side of their foxhole. That night word came to us that one guy was in that foxhole when sand collapsed on top of him. He was buried alive. He was dug out but not before he'd asphyxiated.

Before getting on the jet to come to the Gulf we were issued three sets of auto injector antidote for nerve gas. Part of our training was how to use these auto injector kits in the event of a chemical attack. The injector sets have a one inch needle that is spring loaded. The spring loaded needle shoots out from a protective covering and upon contact injects a nerve agent antidote called atropine. The idea is to grab the injector set and thrust it into the thigh area upon noticing that you've been contaminated with a nerve gas agent. You'd know immediately whether you'd been poisoned by nerve gas. You'd start twitching, sweating, suffocating, farting and pissing all at the same time. You then have about eight seconds to inject yourself with the antidote. If you don't get yourself injected in eight seconds, or there-abouts, you'll either be dead or a twitching vegetable the rest of your life. The spring-action needle is designed to go through thick clothing on contact. We stored the injector sets in our gas mask cases.

In a field environment I can remember using my gas mask case as a pillow many times. It was just about the right size, though not very comfortable. Again, about that third or fourth day at Tent City word came in that somebody had done just that, used their gas mask case as a pillow. The soldier had put pressure enough on the injectors to set one or more of them off directly into his temple area. It killed him quite quickly.

We were not issued the brown desert BDU's when we got to the desert. The army couldn't make enough of them to outfit all the units there. Since the US units from Germany were the last to arrive, we were not issued desert camouflage uniforms until well after the fighting had ceased. It wasn't long, though, before the story started going around that the guys in the green uniforms were the most feared by the Iraqi army; the reason being that we had the more sophisticated M1A1 Abrams tank, as opposed to the older model M1 that most state side units had. The story had its intended effect. We began to think of ourselves as the "bad boys" in green.

The sand killing the guy was a rumor, the atropine in the brain was a rumor, and after everything was over our commanders told us they'd started the story about the Iraqis fearing the "bad boys" in green. Yet all these stories, fact or fiction, had their intended effect. I quit using my gas mask case for a pillow, I didn't dig a foxhole six feet deep, and we were all "baaaaad."

Chow

One of the most enjoyable parts of being at Tent City was the chow. Our food was catered by the same chefs who did the catering for King Faud. The food was good and we got a lot of it; chicken, roast beef, all kinds of American dishes, with the finest of service. The caterers were dressed in fine clothes and served us like we were the king himself. For GI's used to chow and service less than princely, this was some treat. The picture that sticks in my mind of these "Kings Chefs" is being served by them as they held the serving spoon in their right hand, the left behind their back. The Arab custom is to never do anything with the left hand. As this is the hand customarily used to clean oneself after the toilet it is considered an insult to touch anyone or anything with it. The chefs were always at a modified parade rest with that left hand hidden.

There were also private Saudi vendors that came into the area. They had little vans that carried everything from popcorn to the Saudi version of the hamburger and hot dog. We sometimes questioned the meat in these; there were a lot of camels in Saudi Arabia. The vendors also sold the Saudi version of cigarettes. The cigarettes were hand rolled and gave off a spicy scent when smoked. I hadn't smoked regularly for years, but the desert made a lot of us either start the habit or pick up on old habits.

The little Saudi cigarettes, Iraqi tabaccy is what we called them, looked and smelled just a little criminal. They became a fad around Tent City. They were cheap, 50 cents for a pack of 30, so a lot of people were smoking them. One day Captain Hanks walked into the maintenance tent and three or four people were lying back on their cots smoking these thinly rolled, putrid smelling, Saudi cigarettes. It looked and smelled real funny in that tent. The CO looked at the scene a minute and asked if it was a fuckin' party or something? He then threatened to piss test all of us for drugs. He said we might find there was something in those cigarettes we hadn't counted on.

Rain

The second night at Tent City I experienced my first sand storm. The wind blows constantly in the desert, but on frequent occasions it "really" blows. I honestly believe the reason people have been killing each other in the Middle East since the beginning of time is the weather. When I woke up the morning after the sandstorm, I had sand everywhere; in my boots, in my sleeping bag, in all my clothes, in my eyes, in my ears, in my mouth, everywhere. When the wind is blowing in your face and the sand is scraping your skin like a sandblaster, a person can get irritated, very irritated. In January it wasn't hot yet, but combine this with the incredible heat of spring and summer and you have people that just might kill each other over things the rest of the world doesn't quite understand.

Two days after the sand storm it started to rain, and rain, and rain. I don't know the perception people have of the desert, but I know what mine is. Hot and dry, right? The fourth day after my arrival it rained six inches and the temperature dropped to 35 degrees Fahrenheit. The sand quickly became saturated and there was standing water everywhere. It ran into our tent, caving in part of it, and filled up the foxholes we had dug. We managed to get the foxholes bailed out, only to have them fill up again with the next rainstorm a few days later. It got to the point we couldn't bail them out any longer as the rain was steady. We left them full.

It rained hard and on a regular basis for the next two months. I later learned it was the rainiest winter there in many years. I felt the desert should be a green Garden of Eden with the amount of rain that was dumped on us. It was just a little disillusioning. What kind of desert was this?

Speech

About five days before the 15 January UN imposed deadline for Hussein to pull out of Kuwait, we got the lowdown from our NBC (Nuclear, Biological, Chemical) officer on what the big brass felt was going to happen to us, and the Iraqis, in the coming few days. The boys at S-2 (intelligence) said that if Hussein didn't pull out on the

15th, the US would launch air strikes. The Iraqis would probably then launch their Scud missiles on various targets in Saudi Arabia, with Tent City and the port of Dhahran being main targets because of troop and equipment concentration. It dawned on me as I listened to the speech that he was talking about us. We were also told that Hussein might opt for a first strike and that the Scuds were expected to be armed with chemical warheads. We were to expect a chemical attack at anytime from that point until the deadline. If Hussein were to strike with chemical, we were told that US retaliation would be nuclear .... An instant chill went up and down my spine. The S-2 had said these words in a flat monotone; his face showed no emotion. I thought about this briefing a lot in the coming months and to this day find what we were told here hard to believe. But, it is in fact what was said.

The next day we were issued little black radiation detection badges which we attached to our web gear (pistol belt and suspenders which carried a variety of personal military gear) and didn't remove until the end of the war.

The next five days we trained relentlessly for the probable coming attacks. To get used to being in chemical gear for a long period of time we went to MOPP level four, that is, gas mask and all other clothing, for two hours. Having my too small gas mask on my face for two hours was excruciating. A few days after that we went on a land navigation course in MOPP four that lasted about an hour and a half. I feared being in that stuff for a long period of time. In the event of a real chemical attack, where we'd have to wear that equipment for hours or days, I figured I'd for sure become a screaming idiot.

If we came under attack we were to roll out of our bunks, if sleeping, and lie flat on the floor between the cots. After the initial blast, or warning, we would then very quickly get on the gas mask and go to MOPP level four. We would stay in the tents, moving toward the middle as the tent would shield us from falling chemical. The center also provided security from shrapnel if the missiles proved to be conventional.

It was a bit surreal going through all that crazy training in the days before the deadline. We laughed and joked about it a lot. Sergeant Milano and I still didn't believe the crazy bastard was really going to go up against us. It seemed to us a pretty stupid move. I suppose our thinking was reinforced by M1A1 tanks rolling off ships, then driving by our tents all hours of the night. The rumble of a 63 ton tank in the middle of the night has a definite reinforcing feeling.

Deadline

Each passing day brought us closer to the 15 January deadline. It was hard to imagine in those days before the deadline that a real full scale war could start at any hour. During November, 1989 in Germany, the Berlin Wall fell. Being there when it happened was a hell of an experience. I wrote a chapter for this book about going to Berlin after the Wall fell, but left it out figuring it took away from the natural flow of this story. The strange thing about the Wall falling was going outside the next day and finding things in the rest of Germany perfectly normal. Life kept its normal routine, even with chaos and change going on all around us. I thought I should feel or see some momentous shift in my surroundings, but there was none, at least in the part of West Germany we were at. It was that same feeling waiting for the 15 January deadline. Things were very routine. The ships rolled in and we kept training. We were eating good food and even getting hot showers! Life wasn't bad in Tent City.

On the evening of the 14th I was listening to the radio and little good news was being reported. The deadline was only hours away and I knew there was little hope for rationality. I went to sleep with an eye open and my gas mask close at hand.

I slept all night and awoke to a sunny day. There had been such a build up to this date that I expected to wake with the world crashing down around me, instead, I could hear birds chirping while a warm breeze flapped at the sides of the tent. I later saw a comic from a newspaper clipping that showed a husband and wife huddled in front of the television. The caption read "Morning of the 15th of January." The husband is peeking out the curtains and the wife asks if there is anything left.

The whole day of the 15th was calm and normal. We listened to the radio, yet little was being said. With Hussein still in Kuwait the US was saying it had gone through all the negotiations it could. It was an odd day. Hostilities seemed imminent, yet because the weather was nice we played touch football. Everything we did was typical that day, except the feeling of quiet calm. The calm before the storm I suppose.

The 15th passed uneventfully. The morning of the 16th came with more of the same. A big King Faud breakfast, training classes in the morning, break for lunch, more training in the afternoon, then PT (physical training). We were glued to the radio in between. Even less was being said that day on the Armed Forces Network.

"Maybe just nothing gonna happen," Sergeant Milano said between drags on his cigarette.

"I don't know, Sarge. I guess we didn't think about the time difference. We're nine hours ahead of the States here. It's morning there right now and it's dark here."

"Yeah. I suppose all those deadlines were States time. It's just crazy sittin' here waiting like this. The suspense gets to ya, don't it?"

"I don't know what's worse. To sit here and wait or to just get on with it."

"Really seems like it's gonna happen don't it?"

"Yup. Sure does," I said. Sergeant Milano lit up another one of those funny Saudi cigarettes and offered me one. I took it and we smoked in silence.

It was a fairly pleasant dream. I was walking on the beach with a very pretty girl. Then we heard the siren. I looked over to her and asked, "What do you think that is?"

I awoke to flat pitch blackness. The adrenaline pumping instantly. "SCUD LAUNCH, SCUD LAUNCH. WE HAVE SCUD LAUNCH DETECTION. GO TO MOPP LEVEL FOUR."

I found the floor between my cot and the next with a face first thud; the sand an unpleasant late night snack.

Chapter 9
Scud!

The sand was cold, but I didn't feel it. I had nothing on but shorts, dog tags, and a T-shirt. I grabbed for my gas mask. I had strapped it to the front of my cot so I'd know where to find it in the dark. It was on my face, donned and cleared, in a short few seconds. I raised myself out of the sand and sat on the edge of my cot. I checked and rechecked my mask to make damn sure there was absolutely no leakage of outside air through the seals. If this thing was going to work, it had to work now.

Finally someone turned on a flashlight. It was Sergeant Milano next to me as he was getting into the rest of his charcoal chemical suit. He yelled for everyone to do the same. His voice was muffled through the gas mask, but I could hear his heavy breathing. I had to breathe regularly in the constricted gas mask, but the fear made me do otherwise. I started putting on the rest of my chemical gear, the charcoal coat and pants, then socks, combat boots, and the rubber boots that go over the combat boots. The rubber boots seemed to take forever to get on. I moved with a hot, tingly, adrenaline rush of fear. Training gives us eight minutes to put on all that gear. Most everyone did it in about four that night. Sergeant Milano turned on his radio and news reports were saying that huge numbers of fighter jets were leaving bases all over Saudi. I looked at my watch. It was 0150 hours.

After he got his gear on, Sergeant Milano went from man to man, in a frantic manner, making sure everyone's mask was secure (not leaking air). He ran up to every man in the tent, put his hands over the air vents to check the seals, yelling, "Is your masked sealed?! Is your mask sealed?!" It looked funny as I watched him run back and forth like a frantic mother. He was so adamant that a few guys started giving him a hard time, asking if his own mask was sealed. He was looking out after us, but a lot of guys thought he was stirring up fear by running around like that. Keeping your shit together was hard enough as it was.

As we all sat in the tents, waiting for war, the radio began reporting that the skies over Baghdad were being lit by anti-aircraft fire as Allied planes began dropping bombs on targets in and around the city. There was no word on the radio about Scud missile launches, though we continued to be told a launch had been detected. The minutes passed as we sat, listened, and waited. We had previously been issued M-8 and M-9 chemical detection paper, so we began sticking the stuff to our clothing. The paper has a sticky backing and is designed to change color if chemical agent is present in the air. I checked and rechecked the seal on my mask again. Jesus, I wanted a cigarette. About that time a runner from battalion HQ came through the tent door. "Commo! Where the hell is commo?"

"Right here," I said. "What do you want?"

"Colonel Cramer's radio isn't transmitting. He wants commo up there, NOW!"

"What! How come you waited till now to tell me the damn thing ain't working?" I gave the guys from battalion a hard time because most of them knew nothing about operating a radio, except to turn it on, and believe me they could mess that up, too.

"It just went down, man. That's the truth."

Sergeant Milano was still running around checking masks and Sergeant T was in another tent with an advance party getting ready to roll out to our forward area in the desert. I grabbed my tools. "OK. Let's go. Where is he?"

"Just up to battalion, about 200 meters over."

"Jesus help me," I muttered through my mask as I stepped out of the tent. I was walking into a possible chemical missile attack to fix a radio, a radio that most likely had nothing wrong with it as 70% of the time the problem is caused by a radio operator who doesn't know what the fuck he's doing. I was risking my life over transistors and soldered wire!

It was past 0200 hours at this point. I looked around and I saw no one else outside. There were 8000 GI's in tents all around us and we were the only two crazy bastards out walking around! We finally trudged up to battalion HQ. I was sweating like a pig by this time. The chemical suit is a thermal blowtorch inside. There were a few people milling around outside at battalion. This made me feel a little better, but not much. I went to the Colonel's humvee and talked to his driver about what was wrong with the radio. At first I thought it was just a loose cable, but on deeper inspection with my handy test equipment, I could see the radio was fried and needed to be evaced to higher maintenance. I told the driver to bring it by the maintenance tent when he got the chance. In the meantime they would have to pull a radio from a less important vehicle. We did this all the time; shuffle radios back and forth. It was surprising we'd never lost one. I quickly made my exit and trudged the 200 meters back to the maintenance tent. I breathed a sigh of relief as I walked into the relative safety of the tent. Actually, a tent is sure as hell not much protection from a ballistic missile, it just felt better with a roof over my head. Both Sergeant Milano and Sergeant Burgess gave muffled greetings through their masks at my safe return.

Sergeant Burgess

Sergeant Burgess was the maintenance platoon sergeant, the head cheese in maintenance. He was a stout, stocky man, who had been in the army 18 years. He was a seasoned veteran who had seen just about everything there was to see in the army, except maybe a Scud alert.

Sergeant Burgess' cot was right across from mine and we had many conversations about what was going to happen in the coming weeks; especially what would happen if Hussein decided to throw chemical weapons on us. In our conversations it was the opinion of Sergeant Burgess that a chemical war was almost unthinkable. Though the army didn't talk a lot about it, chemical nerve agent can kill in a whole lot of different ways. I can remember him saying he hoped to God Almighty that day never came.

Sergeant Burgess had a director's type folding chair which he sat in while making plans for the coming weeks. That night under our first Scud alert Sergeant Burgess was the slowest man in the tent putting on his chemical gear. As a matter of fact when the battalion runner came in to get me at about ten minutes after the initial alert, Sergeant Burgess still didn't have all his gear on. I remember him sitting in that director's chair calmly taking his time putting on all that equipment. By contrast the rest of us were scared silly. Guys were moving like a film in exaggerated fast motion; gear flying every which way.

Sergeant Burgess was an old soldier who told a lot of stories about life in the army. He knew what the weapons of mass destruction being talked about in this war really meant to us. I'll clarify that and say he knew what our survivability chances were if someone really was going to use them. I wasn't the only person to see old Sergeant Burgess take his time putting on that gear during the first Scud alert. I replayed that scene in my minds eye a lot of times in the coming months. I wondered what the old Sarge knew that the army wasn't talking about, though inside, all of us knew the deal when it came to these weapons .... A lot of poor bastards were gonna die.

About 45 minutes after the initial alert, an "ALL CLEAR" was sounded. We were told to go to MOPP level two (charcoal suit and rubber overboots). I tore the mask from my face and lit a cigarette. Aside from the fact that I was shaky as hell, I felt wide awake. A complete and total awareness had taken over my senses. I could see, hear, and feel everything occurring around me. Everything. I had just learned that fear induced adrenaline is a soldier's most valuable asset. Complete awareness may save your ass in battle. For most of us this first taste of war was the most intense experience of our lives .... Somebody came into the tent and said the Scud missile had fallen short. It was one year later, reading through old newspapers, that I found out no Scuds had been launched that night.

Sergeant Milano had his radio turned up and we were listening to bombing reports as positions in and around Baghdad were hit. Newscasters in Baghdad described the scene as the bombs dropped and the skies lit up with anti-aircraft fire. A real and unreal feeling hit me. It was partly the feeling I had been through this somehow before. I'm sure I had lived it in my dreams a few times. No one seemed very shocked that the bombing was occurring. Maybe we'd all lived it in our dreams. My main thought was here we are, square in the middle of it, and ain't nobody going home soon. A guy by the name of Nellis, from Idaho, said it pretty well. It was shortly after the all-clear had been sounded and we were listening to the radio about the bombing. "If I get out of this thing, and get back to my family, I'm gonna be the kindest, sweetest, gentlest, most loving person on the face of the earth."

Everybody fell quiet after that. It was 0300 hours and wake-up was in two and a half hours. I fell off to sleep quickly, even with all that gear on.

Wake-up was at first light, about 0600 hours. The CO gave us an extra half hour's sleep that day, 17 January, 1991. It was another fair day as the weather during this period had been pretty good. Again, we were glued to news on the radio all day. Wave after wave of bombing sorties were being flown into Baghdad. There was an air base not far from us in Dhahran and I could hear the distant thunder of jets heading to their targets.

Attention to Detail

We again stuck to routine this day, but with the change that we were to go nowhere without gas masks at our side. This had always been stated policy since our arrival in Saudi. As a matter of fact, it had been the policy back in Germany for two months before coming to Saudi. HQ had started this to get us used to the idea of having the thing at our side 24 hours a day. The gas mask policy was being strictly enforced now, and even if we were taking a shower it would not be out of our sight. When I showered I hung it on a nail above the shower door. This made perfect sense to me! I knew exactly where the gas mask was at all times. It was one of the things that I kept constantly reminding myself of.

Keeping track of the gas mask and all the other gear assigned to me was typical of one of the things in army life I had to work at constantly. The army assigns the average combat soldier somewhere in the neighborhood of 100 pounds of basic individual equipment with a value of 1000 dollars or more. Add to this the tools a soldier needs to do his or her job (in my case a tool box of small wrenches and a test set worth 4000 dollars) and a soldier has not only a lot of equipment , but a lot of equipment worth a lot of money.

The most important of all that equipment is the M-16A2 automatic rifle. A lost automatic weapon is a major offense, with a bad conduct discharge or jail as possible consequences. The M-16 is with a soldier 24 hours a day in a field environment, and in our case would be with us for the duration of our stay in the desert. We spent our days with the M-16 and we slept with it at night. The M-16 is your sweetheart. At night I would lay the weapon at my side on the cot, actually sleeping on a corner of it.

Sergeant T told the story of being in a unit where a soldier had lost his M-16 on a field training exercise. The brigade commander held his whole battalion in the field for three extra days because the weapon had not been found. There were a couple of times in my army career when I had to chase down a vehicle because I'd left my weapon inside it while working on a radio. To all of a sudden forget where the hell my weapon was put a lump the size of a football in my gut. I made damn sure I found it in a hurry. First Sergeant Dillon, of Headquarters company, liked to come through the tents at night to see if he could walk out with someone's weapon. I guess he did this to keep us on our toes.

First Sergeant Dillon was not well liked in the company. He came from the mortar platoon where he'd done such a poor job as platoon sergeant, someone decided he should be promoted to company first sergeant. Hard to figure how some things work in the army. There's an old army saying, though, and it holds true in this case. "Fuck up, move up." The main problem with First Sergeant Dillon was that he was incompetent. An added problem to that was that he knew we knew he was incompetent. He was the one leader out of all the others who provoked fear in me. The story about him was that he had the mortar platoon lost for two days on a training exercise in Germany because he couldn't read a map. Captain Hanks, his boss, certainly could read a map, and as long as he was around we were alright. First Sergeant Dillon became a scary character, though, if for some reason Captain Hanks wasn't around.

Keeping track of all that personal equipment, then, was a hell of a job; one I had to train my mind to do on a daily, even hourly basis. When I was sitting doing nothing I would go over in my head where all my equipment was, every piece of it, and if it was secure. Every little item had to be accounted for. Perfect attention to detail. "Perfect, perfect, perfect."

A Jillion Fishes

In those days we did a lot of our training on the seawall that separated Tent City from the Persian Gulf. The seawall was a man-made dike of huge boulders, rocks, and sand that ran along the north and west perimeter of Tent City. The top of this 15 foot embankment was large enough for tanks and Bradleys to perch upon and keep watch for the Iraqi U-boats that may have been out there.

On nicer days we'd take our training breaks sitting on the rocks that led down to the blue-green water of the Gulf. On one of those days a buddy in my platoon by the name of Jimmy Dudley, and myself, were having a conversation. Jimmy "D" was a small statured black man, no more than 5 feet 4 inches tall, with a friendly, outgoing manner. He was also a natural comedian. He had a sense of humor that put me, and most people in the maintenance platoon, into fits of laughter. "D" also made fun of his size by acting like the baddest cat on the block; and he could pull it off. Many a day he'd walk up to company formations, or whatever, shoulders rotating back and forth as he walked, giving his bad-ass stare, telling us he was our worst nightmare.

It was funny as hell cause he knew it was funny.

That day when "D" and I were talking, a black cloud seemed to come to the shore of the sea, stretching out about 100 meters up and down the seawall. It was a massive school of fish and we watched as the gulls snapped up one after another. I told "D" there must have been a jillion fishes out there.

"D" gave a slow chuckle. "I never heard of the number jillion before there, "J"." As with the rest of army jargon, a lot of us were simply known by a letter of the alphabet; Sergeant T, Dudley, myself. "That's what you think, though. A jillion of those fishes, ha?"

"Yeah, "D". At least a jillion. Maybe more."

From that time on whenever things got a little slow, and "D" would catch sight of me, he'd bring up the topic about the size of the number jillion. I guess "D" thought that was the funniest number he'd ever heard and he badgered me relentlessly to tell him just how big a number jillion was. It was an honor to be made fun of by "D". There aren't many people who can make fun of you and make you feel good while they're doing it. "D" had a gift. He is probably the funniest man I've ever met.

Anyway, about that number jillion. "Webster's Dictionary" defines jillion as, "A large indeterminate number." There you go, "D".

The Pill

Another routine that started the first night of the air war was taking the little white pill. The pill was a pre-antidote to nerve agent poisoning. When we were awoke for the Scud launch warning we were told to go to MOPP level four and to take a pill. We carried two packets of 25 or 30 pills in our gas mask cases. The dosage was one pill every eight hours in the event of an expected chemical attack. There was talk of experimental drugs being issued to us. We were told the pre-antidote for nerve agent poisoning was not experimental, so we all took it dutifully. If it wasn't experimental, then, I wondered who the guys were that had tested this thing.

When I first took this pill I felt a bit of a tingly feeling all over. By the time the next morning came .... well, let's just say I had to shit. Bad. I went over to use the latrines and I had to wait in line. Everybody had to shit. We had to take the pill for three straight days during this period. It was three days of nausea. The drug evidently opened nerve endings in our bodies. This would make it easier for the real antidote (the atropine injectors we carried in our gas mask cases) to reach our nerves if we had to us it. We were told the drug would open us up; clean us out so to speak. Nobody was kidding about that.

"SCUD LAUNCH! SCUD LAUNCH! GO TO MOPP LEVEL FOUR! MOPP LEVEL FOUR!" I was awake in an instant. Again, it was pitch black in the tent, and it seemed I'd just fallen off to sleep.

"Alright! Get up and get the shit on!" somebody yelled.

"Just like last night!" Nellis blurted out before he threw on his gas mask.

"I know the son-of-a-bitch's plan," I thought out loud, the words muffled through my mask. "The idea is to keep us up every goddamn night with a Scud launch."

Sergeant Burgess gave a belly shaking laugh as he sat in his usual position across from me in the directors chair. Everyone else was going through the same hurried routine as last night, but there was Sergeant Burgess in that relaxed position taking his time. "Yup. A few wars been won because one side never let the other get any sleep."

"Israel's being hit with Scuds," Sergeant Milano reported. He turned up the radio and we heard the sirens of Tel-Aviv come over the airwaves.

We listened and waited.

"B-O-O-M B-O-O-M!" Two thundering crashes shook the air above the tent; loud enough to physically shake the fabric of our dwelling and the ground under our feet. The hot rush of fear I'd felt last night again enveloped my head, surging through me; an already familiar feeling.

"What the fuck was that?" Sergeant Milano's yell was muffled by his gas mask.

"What the fuck you think it was!" Nellis yelled back.

"Sounded like the real fucking thing to me!"

I looked down at the chemical detection paper stuck to my chemical protective suit. Again, I checked my mask seal, contemplating the unthinkable. It became quiet, only the radio blurted noise as we waited. I remember thinking it was strange to have instant access to what was going on in this war. For people back home the war was happening on their television screens the moment it occurred. For us in the tents, CNN was telling us who Scuds were being launched at, and that miraculously some were being intercepted by Patriot missiles! This information came to us well before our commanders could know what was happening .... The seconds, and then minutes, ticked past. Finally, about 30 minutes after the explosions, an all-clear was given. The radio reported two Scuds fired at General Schwarzkopf's central command in Riyahd, Saudi Arabia, had been intercepted by Patriot missiles. It also reported one Scud had been fired at us here in Dhahran and had also been intercepted by the Patriot. It was unclear how many had been fired into Israel. I wondered why I'd heard two booms and later learned that the Patriot first breaks the sound barrier then explodes; hopefully taking an incoming missile with it.

We were told that satellite reconnaissance would give us ten minutes warning in the event of another launch and that we should get some sleep. Daybreak was in an hour.

Patriot!

"The Patriot? I thought that was an air defense missile for taking out jets," said Nellis. Nellis slept in the cot next to me at Tent City. He had these thick lensed glasses he was virtually blind without. We'd always gotten along well; until now when we had to live next to each other.

"I guess it can take out the missiles, too," Sergeant Burgess scratched his rather large belly. "I don't think many countries knew we had such a thing. There's a whole battery just a half mile up the road here."

Sergeant Milano was in the corner smoking a Kool and listening to the news. "I didn't know it could do that either. Man, that has to be some serious technology, ha?"

"Hard to imagine something could be that exact. I mean, hit a missisle going how many thousands of miles an hour? Big time." I said.

Talk of Patriot this and Patriot that was all over the news that morning. The story of Scuds being blown out of the sky the night before was a big hit. Also the news reported that all Scuds fired here, Riyahd, and into Israel were conventional. There had been no release of chemical in any of these areas. We breathed a little easier.

Spades

It was about 1900 hours that evening, 18 January, and most of us had just finished some good King Faud chow and were relaxing in the tents. I found this to be the best part of the day at Tent City. Early evenings just after chow were a good time to write letters home, do some reading, or just have some conversation. A game of spades had started in the middle of the tent. Sergeant Burgess, Nellis, Cook (the platoon artist), and usually Sergeant Milano would play cards about every night. Tonight, though, Sergeant Milano was writing in a note-book in the corner of the tent, and listening to the radio. They were talking about Israeli civilians going into shelters; mothers and kids wearing gas masks.

The card game kept going and every once in a while Nellis, or somebody else, would yell over and want to know what was happen-ing. A newsman described how last night the people had to put on their gas masks and go to secured rooms because no one knew if the Scuds carried chemical weapons. The fact that Hussein bombed innocent civilians in a country not directly involved in the conflict was all over the news. I kept thinking how terrified I had been the last two nights, and I train for this shit. Now regular folks, and kids, had to do the same thing. I could not imagine it.

"The guy is a gangster, man," I said to Sergeant Milano, looking up from the letter I was writing back home. "Did you know his favor-ite books are about Chicago mobs of the 1920's? What can you expect from somebody like that?"

"I just can't believe he's shooting missiles at innocent people, and kids."

"I think it's pretty obvious the guy's just a little off his rocker. He didn't back down when we though he would. It's hard to predict what he's capable of."

Sergeant Milano wrote children's books in his spare time. He kept a journal, writing his stories in longhand. He looked up, "I don't know what I'd do if it was my kids having to put on a gas mask and run down to the cellar. What kind of man can do that, "J"?"

"I don't know, Sarge ...."

"Whose deal is it?" somebody yelled from the card game .... I listened as the dealer shuffled and the cards were dealt.

Chapter 10
Roll Out

There were many more Scud alerts in the one week's time we had left in Tent City, the most memorable coming five days after the beginning of the war. It was early in the morning, about 0700 hours, and I was at the mess tent eating a good hardy breakfast, compliments of the king. Just as I got my food, two earth moving B-O-O-M B-O-O-M's crashed over top of the mess tent. I left my food where it was and threw on my gas mask. The kings chefs had their own little gas masks and were throwing them on in a hurry like the rest of us, but they at least had the brains to stay put! There were about 500 GI's in the mess tent and everybody was running outside and back to their tents. Pretty dumb thing to do when I look back. How did we know what was outside? At least the mess tent had the cover of canvass. As I ran back to the maintenance tent, I looked up into a cloudless blue morning sky where two large white puffs of smoke could be seen with two long trails of the same coming down to earth. I was struck immediately by the similarity of the smoke and trailing clouds, to pictures of the explosion of the space shuttle Challenger. The Patriots had done their job, as I was witnessing the remnants of two Iraqi Scuds. What I couldn't believe, though, was how far away the smoke seemed. It was many thousands of feet into the air. The Patriot intercepting the Scud created one hell of an explosion. The violent ear-splitting noise of those interceptions sounded, and felt, like they were directly overhead.

On the 20th of January the first ship with Red Lion equipment arrived in port. The arrival was about one week late due to a storm on the North Sea and mechanical problems on two of the ships. The journey for our equipment, trucks, and tanks had started in early December when we drove the trucks and other "wheeled" vehicles to Mannheim, Germany where they were loaded on barges and shipped up the Rhine River to ports in northern Europe. The tanks and other "track" type vehicles were loaded on Bundesbahn (German Rail) cars at the Rock, and taken to the ports. Now, 45 days later, they had arrived in Saudi Arabia. I was amazed at how well the system worked. After experiencing army bureaucracy move like a snail 90% of the time, it was incredible to see its ability to move this mass of men and equipment.

In the ports of Dhahran there were freighters from all over the world: Italian ships, Egyptian ships, South American ships from Brazil and Argentina. One day a French destroyer came into port and docked. Dog and Sergeant Smith rode with our equipment in a Greek freighter. When they arrived they told the story of the storm on the North Sea and three days of sea-sickness; of being on the Mediterra-nean and going through the Suez Canal; of stopping in Egypt. An adventure like this in the hands of Dog, though, took on epic propor-tions:

"And you should have seen those Egyptian women. Oh, man, they were fiiiiiine!" Dog had a way of stretching out that word fine. Ole' Dog had been in the service quite a few years and had travelled all around the world. He would have long discussions and arguments comparing one type of woman's features to another. I would call Dog a master analyst when it came to the female of the species.

The day the first of our ships steamed into port I was assigned to a detail team unloading trucks and equipment from it. I gladly took this assignment because the bowels of those great ships was something I had to see. My basic job was to drive vehicles from the ship to the parking areas along the port. About halfway through the day I got the chance to go inside and unhook chains that held the vehicles to its deck. It was hard work unhooking and hauling the heavy chains. The sound of men yelling and vehicle chains slamming to the deck echoed throughout the cavernous spaces of the freighter. The size of the ship was impressive indeed. From the dock I had paced the length of it at 300 feet. It held hundreds of trucks, trailers, and humvees.

At the end of that day I had a conversation with one of the men directing the unloading. He spoke in awe of this massive movement of men and equipment. He had arrived in port on November 15th. That day in January he was unloading his 95th ship.

One of the first tasks at hand was to give a new paint job to the wheeled and track vehicles. Everything coming off the ships had green jungle camouflage paint. This was fine in the woods of Germany, not in the desert. Green was out, brown was in. Painting sheds worked round the clock in what proved to be a huge operation. Due to a lack of time, and I'm sure paint, only combat vehicles like tanks, Bradleys, apc's (armored personnel carriers), commander's humvees, and trucks that would be near the front received the sand paint jobs. I hoped this was a good decision because the vehicle I would be in was none of the above. I reminded myself of the story where the Iraqis thought the guys in green were the real bad dudes.

After the paint jobs the vehicles had to be inspected for mechanical soundness. Within the next four or five days we would be driving 250 miles through the desert to a place called TAA (Tactical Assembly Area) Henry, and there was a lot of work to do. After sitting on ships for 45 days there were bound to be some problems. Myself, Sergeant T, and Sergeant Milano began a full maintenance inspection of every radio in Headquarters company. There were three of us and 165 radios, all with various antenna and intercom systems. In four days all of it had to be in perfect working order.

I have yet to comment on the equipment I worked with. The fact of the matter is that most of it was old and outdated. Vietnam era communications equipment was used in most tactical vehicles in our battalion. My job was to work in state of the art million dollar tanks and Bradley's, on radio equipment worth what we jokingly figured to be 30 dollars! The army spent a lot of money on their tanks and weapons, but forgot about upgrading the commo. The importance of communications between vehicles in a combat situation goes without saying, yet oftentimes the age of the equipment we worked on made the systems unreliable. Lt. Colonel Cramer was on our asses constantly about his radios. The equipment required a hell of a lot of maintenance and sometimes just plain willpower to keep it working. I began to see articles in the Stars and Stripes newspaper telling of commanders complaining about vehicle to vehicle tactical communications not being up to par. They were right. It was my job to keep that old equipment alive.

Fiery Debris

During the next few days I had a chance to go all over the port areas of Dhahran. One of the things that caught my eye was the incredible amount of munitons (tank rounds, artillery rounds, and more), that were stored in huge open shelters at various places in the port. After all the Scud alerts we had gone through in the last few days, I thought about the possibility of just one Scud missile hitting those munitions. Half the port would go up.

About two days after the equipment arrived I was working at the dock areas where the vehicles were parked. About 1700 hours I

83

jumped on a shuttle bus back to Tent City. Things were progressing routinely as far as commo was concerned so I was able to get most of my work done during daylight hours. While driving along the coastal highway that looked out over the Gulf there was a hell of an explosion overhead. By that time everybody knew what that meant so we threw on our gas masks. When we arrived back at Tent City the all-clear had been given so I headed to the maintenance tent. Sergeant T was there to greet me.

"Jesus, I'm glad to see you here! We were outside the tent when the Patriot slammed that Scud! Blew the shit out of it then parts of missile started landing on the dock areas." Sergeant T was talking fast and pointing to the area I had been working in that day. His eyes were big gray marbles magnified by his thick glasses.

"I was just working over there, Sarge! We heard the explosion on the bus during the trip back here."

"No shit, Sherlock. I know you were working over there. I'm the guy who sent you over there, remember?"

I was so relieved to be in one piece I thought the remark was pretty funny. "Oh, yeah. Sure Sergeant T. I guess you did send me over there today."

"Yeah." He stopped. I saw those owl eyes get even bigger. "Smartass. Anyway, it looked to me like those fragments landed right on the dock parking lots. I wonder if anybody got hit by that shit?"

"There's just tons of ammo over there, Sarge. Jesus, there'd be one hell of an explosion if that shit was hit."

We waited for news about damage to that area or injuries to people over there, but nothing was ever heard about it. The docks where the missile fragments seemed to land was about two miles from Tent City. Eventually we figured the illusion of distance made it seem like the fragments dropped on the dock parking lots, but they probably fell into the sea. The Cement City and MGM Grand troop housing areas were just the other side of the docks where the fragments seemed to land. There were thousands of US troops in these areas. The scene was an eerie preview to the future. Patriots were apparently blowing Scuds out of the sky left and right, but what was left after the explosions had to come down somewhere.

After all the tanks and other track vehicles had been painted and inspected, it was time for them to be loaded aboard huge transport trucks and driven to our desert assembly location. As the track vehicles were being loaded and trucked, the rest of us started getting our equipment and other belongings ready for the long trip.

I was driving HQ-37. In the past this humvee had been assigned to commo maintenance and Sergeant T, but when Colonel Cramer arrived in Saudi he reassigned the vehicle. Before coming to the desert Sergeant T and I set about building shelves and making other modifications on the vehicle to get it ready. With the way things were changing on a daily and even hourly basis, though, we should have known it wouldn't last. About a week after our arrival in country, battalion decided 37 should go back to the wireteam at battalion commo. Battalion commo, as opposed to Headquarters company commo (of which me and Sergeant T were a part), had a total of six people. The Lieutenant, a comsec specialist (communications security), and four wiredogs. Their job was not to fix radios, but to oversee the day to day operations of battalion communications as a whole. They had recently been assigned a four man wireteam. In the past Headquarters commo had taken care of wire communications (telephone) with the manpower we had. An armored battalion is by nature highly mobile and the need to string wire for stationary telephones is limited. We rely mainly on the airwaves. Yet the army and our battalion commander, in a stroke of brilliance, had decided to create this second layer of bureaucracy. They then assigned this bureaucracy four new "wiredogs" just before the war. Essentially, the four wiredogs had no job to do. But, since there were four of them, they of course needed a vehicle. We asked what job it was the wiredogs would do and the answer was string wire. Army doctrine said we were to be assigned a wire-team and they were to get a vehicle. That was that. The system was awe-inspiring at times.

Tap Line Road

It was 2300 hours, 24 January, 1991. Our vehicles were lined up in convoy formation ready to roll. The main road to our assembly area, Tap Line Road, was reported to be a dangerous, rough piece of highway. There was myself and three of the wiredogs in HQ-37. Even though Sergeant T and I were supposed to be assigned this vehicle, I couldn't hold it against the wiredogs. They were all pretty good guys. It wasn't their fault they were assigned to a unit with no job to do. They were named Jackson and Morris, with another guy they just called Splinter, like the rat leader of the Teenage Mutant Ninja Turtles (a popular kids cartoon at the time). They claimed he looked just like that rat.

About 2400 hours we started our roll-out. The first part of the journey was through the wide freeways around Dhahran, but it wasn't long before the highway narrowed and turned into a two lane road. The claim that Tap Line Road was dangerous was no joke. The military traffic going both ways was constant, night and day. The biggest problem were the huge transport trucks hauling tanks and other armored vehicles. Their width had me hugging the far right shoulder of the road to avoid them as they took up more than their fair share of highway. Mangled trucks, humvees, and civilian automobiles littered the side of the highway. The sight of those crash scenes every few miles kept me on my toes. Losing concentration could be deadly. More than a couple GI's had bitten the dust on this highway. The traffic, even in the early hours before daylight, was bumper to bumper.

As the first part of the trip was at night, I saw what looked like oil storage tanks burning in the distance. These were somehwere in between the cities of Jubail and Khafji, about 50 miles or so from Dhahran. The Iraqi's had made artillery attacks on refineries in this area and I believed I was seeing the fiery results in the distance. A buddy from the 3rd of the 5th Cavalry Battalion, a unit in my brigade, had come to Saudi in one of the advance parties to construct facilities for the coming troops. He worked in the port city of Jubail, a completely new city constructed by the Bechtel Corporation of San Francisco. It is hard to imagine building a completely new city from the ground up, but that is what Jubail is.

As daylight approached, the traffic, which I didn't think could get any heavier, did. I was able to get my first look at the small towns and desert villages of rural Saudi Arabia. These were more like the pictures I had in my mind of the desert Middle East. Compared to the gleaming new cities along the Persian Gulf, the rural towns are shabby and dirty. In the desert sand surrounding the towns I saw the trash of civilization thrown haphazardly over the ground. Junk cars littered the streets. The buildings in the villages were ancient, sand brown, adobe like structures. Between them were electric utility poles and parked on the streets were many brand new Nissan pickup trucks. The contrast between ancient and modern was striking.

Tap Line Road was named for the large oil pipeline that straddled the south side of the highway. That pipeline made me think about the reason I was in this place. It carried huge amounts of liquid energy, from a place with more of that liquid energy than anywhere on earth. The commander in chief talked a lot about freeing oppressed people, and of course this was true, but that was one very big pipeline.

After driving all night I let Jackson take the wheel. I relaxed and tried to get a little sleep. The 250 mile trip would take almost 18 hours as the traffic made speeds very slow at times. Jackson, Morris, and Splinter had been with one of the Pershing missile units in Germany before the INF (International Nuclear Forces) treaty with the Soviets closed down their base. After the closure these guys were just extra personnel. That's how they ended up in a tank battalion. Jackson said he'd figured on going back to the States when the base closed, but instead, whammo, he ended up in the desert. Jackson was trying to make his sergeant's stripes, like myself. The end of the Cold War was making that a tough task. It was a strange situation. On the one hand there was a great deal of talk about cutbacks in personnel and promotions, but on the other soldiers were being held in the army beyond the ETS (end of service) dates because of war in the Gulf. We had six or seven guys in Headquarters company that had their ETS date extended indefinitely. They weren't happy campers. Some had been scheduled to get out of the army just days before troops started being sent to the Gulf.

About 1400 hours that day signs said the King Khalid Military City (KKMC) was just up the road. KKMC was a sprawling Saudi Arabian military complex that rivaled any American base. TAA Henry was not far from KKMC, so I knew we were close. Across from the entrance to KKMC we turned from the blacktop highway and headed into the desert. Different colored barrels marked the incredibly rutted desert path for the next 30 miles. Red barrels in the road marked the way to and from KKMC, blue for division HQ, and so on. Since we'd had so much rain during the last few weeks the road was a trenched and rutted hellhole. As my kidneys rattled inside me and my lower back vertebrae were compressed from flying close to the ceiling and slamming back to the seat a time or two, I knew the reality of desert life was about to strike. The makeshift road we were on was a half mile wide, with a new path carved out of the desert every time it had rained. Evidently this was an actual Saudi road. About 15 miles into the desert we made a sharp turn to the south, and at that corner was a little village settlement. It sat on a little knoll with high adobe buildings at its edge; like a small fortress. The gray sky that day made it a bleak picture; desert brown wasteland in the foreground of a lonely little outpost. A little town on the edge of the world.

There was an oasis on the desert trail to our assembly area. Trees had sprouted around it. Some of the trees looked like pine or spruce, but I'm sure they were some variety I was not familiar with. Every once in a while a trademark red and white Nissan pickup truck went tearing by us; the standard mode of modern transport for the rural Saudi people. Most of the people in this area were Bedouins, the travelling nomads of desert lore. Their tents could occasionally be seen in the distance. Their camels grazed on the few grassy areas that had sprung from the recent rains. I got my first look at the camel. Upon closer inspection in the days to come it seemed their faces always had a wry smile. Like, "the joke's on you buddy," for being in a place like this.

Finally we arrived at a hollowed out valley with windswept rock and sandy dunes surrounding it. This was TAA Henry. It reminded me of a dugout quarry common in the countryside where I'm from back in the States. Headquarters company of the Red Lion battalion occupied the little hollowed out cove we had come upon. It hid our company so well I couldn't see any part of it until I was right on the place. The barren hills in this part of the desert had the advantage of breaking the incessant winds somewhat. With a blowing wind open desert is murder. As I stepped out of the hummer that wind was blowing fast. A little swirl picked up sand, blowing it into my eyes, welcoming me to the desert.

Chapter 11
TAA Henry

The first thing we did after arriving at TAA henry was get our living arrangements in order; get a roof over our heads. As we arrived in camp it was a nasty, windy day with darkness just an hour away. The battalion had acquired a bunch of small, four man Saudi army tents which were fairly quick and easy to set up, so we went to work. They were like the Bedouin tents we'd seen in the desert; white or yellow in color with a high pitched roof and four sides, perfectly square. They looked like they'd been in storage for some time as the ropes used to tie them down were frayed, some broke as we pulled them to tighten the tents. They were fairly sound, though, without many holes.

As we struggled with the canvass a feeling of emptiness filled the pit of my stomach. I felt like a child lost in the wilderness. I'd entered a hollow void; I was completely alone. "Jesus, what am I doing here?" I asked Him. I knew I had to repress these feelings. Darkness would not envelop me. I'd had these empty moments before; on other moves to strange places with the army.

With darkness approaching fast and a stiff north wind that promised a storm, we struggled to put up the tents. The wind blew sand in my face and eyes, stinging fiercely, the tears ran trying to flush it out. We had goggles for driving and if guys had a pair they put them on. Everyone would be issued goggles. In a sandstorm I could not walk outside without them. Sergeant T, myself, and a wheels mecha- nic named Ronson worked to set up a tent for ourselves. Just after nightfall we had it done. It wasn't much, but it had four walls and was enough to keep out the wind and rain. The sprinkles from the coming storm were just starting. There was hot chow that night at the mess the battalion cooks had set up, making the hole in my stomach smaller.

We were told this was the one hot meal we would get per day, the rest would be rations; MRE's. After the late chow I set up my cot and sleeping bag, it had been a long day. Stand-to was at 0500 hours. That's when we'd start digging in.

Stand-To

It was an 0430 wake-up to a morning of blustery rain and temperatures in the 30's. We were told that average daily temperatures in the desert interior would be 20 or 30 degrees cooler than along the Persian Gulf in Dhahran. When I stuck my head out of my sleeping bag that morning, I knew I hadn't been lied to. It was tough getting the nerve to crawl out into that cold, wet air. Crawling out of a snug, warm sleeping bag into a cold morning is the worst part of being in the field. On the other hand, crawling into that warm bag at night is about the best. At least the tent hadn't leaked. The Saudi tents looked pretty shabby, but they were water tight.

At 0500, after I'd gotten on my gear, (rain jacket, pants, and boots) Ronson and I headed into the dark morning to find a spot for stand-to guard. We took a hilltop just above where the tents had been set up. The spot was on the edge of the hill, overlooking the desert in an easterly direction. We brought shovels and a pick-ax and started digging. Stand-to was two hours in the morning and two hours in the evening, every day. The idea is to be on alert one hour before sunrise and one hour after; in the evenings it was one hour before sunset and one hour after. These are, according to the army, the best times for an enemy attack. Though we ran 24 hour guard shifts at the gates to the assembly area and certain posts around the perimeter, every member of the battalion took part in stand-to. Stand-to happened every single day, before, during, and after the hostilities.

Doing the digging that first morning at least kept us warm. Any guard duty was usually extremely boring and damn cold. There just isn't a lot of physical activity while on guard. At least we had something to do this first morning; dig a hole four feet long, two feet wide and three feet deep. Ronson and I were glad to do it.

Ronson was the kind of guy who thought everything in the world had some humor in it. The guy had a great attitude all the time, sometimes to my irritation. I mean, I just had a hard time being cheerful when I was in a hole in the desert, cold, with rain pouring down on me one minute and sand blowing in my eyes the next. Ronson always had an amusing anecdote or upbeat saying. Anyway, after digging for two hours and listening to a few bad jokes, we had a pretty good hole dug, even though we had to pick-ax every inch. Contrary to my belief that the desert was nothing but sand, I found that just a little bit of sand blew back and forth covering the desert with only a few inches of the stuff; the rest is rock.

It was chilly and wet that first morning, but it was nothing compared to a morning I remember well in the first week of February. I awoke for stand-to on this morning and when I stuck my head out of the bag it was cold, real cold. I threw on my clothes fast, then started digging into my gear for every piece of cold weather clothing I could find. I was damn happy I'd heeded advice and brought the stuff with me. When I packed I remember thinking I'd probably not need it. Baloney. When I stepped outside that morning there was frost on the ground, the only time I remember seeing that in the desert. It was damn cold up in the hole. Ronson and I kept up a conversation between chattering teeth. Just below freezing isn't all that cold, but add in a stiff wind and believe me the wind chill was below zero. We got down in the three foot hole as far as we could, while still peeking over the top to keep an eye out. Yeah, we remembered our duty, even while freezing.

I hadn't heard of anyone being attacked by Iraqi troops in this part of Saudi yet, though the battle of Khafji, in which Iraqi troops crossed the border of Kuwait into Saudi attacking this abandoned oil refining city and marine positions there, had occurred about this time. At TAA Henry we were about 100 miles from Kuwait and Khafji. 100 miles isn't that far away. We kept a vigil. One other thing I remember about that morning, besides the cold, was the incredible sunrise. Perfectly clear skies had driven the temperatures way down and when the sun rose in the east over the frost covered desert, the sand and hills were transformed. A pristine wasteland; beautiful for a short period. The frost, like a prism, seemed to split the light into its various colors. Purple, red, and yellow shown off the rolling dunes. I looked over at the rest of the guys in the platoon crouched in holes around us, the fur lined cold weather gear making us look like arctic explorers. At 0700 as stand-to came to an end, I popped out my camera and shot pictures of us all. Without pictures I figured no one back home would ever believe me when I told them the desert got that cold.

MRE's

After stand-to it was time for breakfast; rations, MRE's, the army's Meals Ready to Eat. We had other terms for them, such as Meals Rejected by Ethiopia, which was partly true. The government had tried to send some of these to drought stricken African countries and they'd been sent back.

The MRE is the ultimate in modern prepackaged food technology. There are 12 different varieties of the MRE ranging from spaghetti to chicken-a-la-king to ham slices to omelettes. The main meal is usually sealed in an airtight packet and is precooked to be eaten cold, or can be warmed for a hot meal. In my army experience I have never eaten any other kind of basic ration. The C-ration of Vietnam fame is what the MRE replaced. From soldiers who have experienced both rations it is said the C-ration was better, the MRE more convenient.

A typical MRE is made up of the main meal packet, a second packet such as au-gratin potatoes, and other items such as crackers, peanut butter, and jelly. There's a dessert like applesauce, a cookie or candy bar, and a packet of personal items such as toilet paper, wet towelettes, matches, gum, salt, sugar, and instant coffee. Later versions of the MRE came with a Kool Aid mix. The army claims there are 3000 calories in each MRE. I could rarely finish all the food in one sitting. It wasn't that I wasn't hungry; it's just that after the first time I'd eaten, or experienced, all the different varieties of MRE, I simply could stand no more. Eating them day after day isn't any fun. If they are heated they are much better, but often we had no chance to heat them.

While I was losing weight because of the monotony of the diet, there were a few, two people in particular, who actually were gaining weight from the MRE's. Since two of our meals every day were MRE's, the guys with the iron stomachs were getting fat. We joked about it because the two people we saw gaining weight were the two old time sergeants; Sergeant T, and Sergeant Burgess. These guys had been in the army so long I guess they'd learned how to eat army rations and like it. Then, on the other hand, it could have been the cookies from home. Sergeant Burgess was a cookie monster. The man had a way of getting a few cookies out of every guy's care package. Since he handed out the mail he knew if a soldier had gotten cookies or other food from home, then he went to work figuring how to get some of it. In his humvee he had three or four different types of cookies stashed in various parts of the vehicle; Oreos, Fig newtons, somebody's mom's chocolate chip. Being in charge gives a man leverage. Maybe a guy needed a ride to the post exchange at division HQ, or the phones to call home. A half bag of chocolate chip. No problem.

The care packages from people back home were great. When our mail started finally coming through, which was about a month after we'd arrived in country, we were getting all kinds of "any serviceman" letters. To be nice we tried to write people back in our spare time. One of the letters I answered was from a young couple in Minneapolis. Since that was pretty much home for me I wrote them that I was from that area and thanked them for the letter. In the next three months I received four big one pound freezer bags full of chocolate chip cookies.

Back to the MRE. The first few days of a consistent MRE diet isn't bad. But after a week the digestive track takes a definite turn toward the stoppage mode. The food seems to slow to a halt the whole digestive system. It must be the preservatives, or maybe it's just part of the genius behind whoever puts these things together, but I've known guys who didn't have a bowel movement for 15 days because of a steady MRE diet. A person could explode. Literally.

Settling In

After getting our living arrangements straight, and dug in, we started situating ourselves; getting used to day to day life in the desert. In early February mail finally started arriving on a regular basis. The mail service was extremely slow, but I had no problems with lost mail, though I did get late word that my sister had had a baby. I knew she was due the first week of January, but I didn't find out until almost mid

February. After I'd found out I was a new uncle I had Cook, the artist, make up a card. A bunch of guys in the platoon signed it.

January 27, 1991
Dear Family,

I am finally out at our desert location. We arrived here on the 25th. There is very little here except sand and there is a pile of that! I was happy to leave Dhahran as there were many Scud missile alerts there. The Patriot missile definitely did its job as there were fireworks when those babies took them out. Anyway, things are much quieter here. We are between 65 and 100 miles from Kuwait and very isolated. I do not know when we are moving but will probably be soon.

My mail situation is terrible. I've gotten one package so far. I do not know about the baby as I have no other letters yet.

Very cold and rainy today. Some days are nice, but I can't believe how much rain they are getting here. Am staying busy with radio work and such. We do have portable showers but am waiting for it to warm up. Had a shower four days ago which ain't bad. We get one hot meal a day so that's not bad either. The rest are the infamous MRE's. Maybe you've heard about these. M-M-Good!

Well, I wanted to write and let you know we made it to this location and all is quiet. Will write again when I hopefully get mail. May get to a telephone in a few days, we'll see. Have not seen one yet, but evidently they are around here. See you soon.

Love
Carey

After a week or so the tanks and other equipment started arriving and we began our day to day maintenance routines, getting vehicles and equipment ready for the grueling desert. We started preparing for a training exercise that would take us out in a mock roll-out through the desert. The idea was to learn the types of formations we would use for the seemingly inevitable ground offensive into Kuwait. It would be a three day roll-out and would be the first test of equipment performance, the different formations, and how well the command structure was going to work. Our job in commo had been pretty routine to this point. The work we had done at port was holding up .... so far.

Desert Test

We rolled out on the exercise early in the a.m. on the 8th of February. The exercise was run by each battalion in our brigade individually. We were told the real thing would be in brigade sized elements, about six times as large.

The weather had turned sunny during those days and it was nice not to have the rain to contend with. Without rain, though, the desert turns to dust instantly. There were enough vehicles in our battalion size formation to raise one hell of a dust storm. When all the vehicles were moving at once I simply kept an eye on the vehicle to my front because that is all I could possibly see. If we lost sight of that vehicle it could get wild as trucks moved to the sides and rear. The best idea was to travel in the tracks. As a matter of fact, traveling outside the tracks would be fatal during the real thing. As long as I wasn't the first vehicle cutting the path I wouldn't hit a land mine. A person might ask about that first vehicle; it was a tank.

We moved out in a V-type formation. We were actually borrowing Soviet tactics here as the wedge type V is Soviet tank doctrine.

98

It was perfect for the wide open desert. The V-type formation is like its name. It consists of a unit of M1A1 tanks taking the middle point. Flanking to the rear on both sides are two other units of tanks. Straggling along both sides of the formation from front to rear is a mix of tanks, Bradley fighting vehicles, air defense artillery such as the Vulcan machine gun and Chaparral missile system, and infantry troops in armored personnel carriers. Multiple launch rocket systems and 155 mm self propelled howitzer field artillery are out there also. In my observations the multiple launch guys were to the sides and the howitzer guys were more toward the front areas. This V leaves the whole middle open and hopefully protected on all sides. In the middle the command and control vehicles travel with all other support elements. In a brigade sized support element, the typical size for combat support, there are up to 1000 vehicles. I rode in the center of the V along with fuelers, ammo carriers, duece-and-a-half troop carriers, hummers, recovery vehicles, and medical personnel.

Bedouins

As the battalion moved through the desert on our training mission I had a chance to see the Bedouins close up. I wondered what they thought as all those men, women (there were many females in the combat support units traveling right along with us), and machines rolled by their camps. What I remember most about those camps were the children. There were always a whole bunch of kids since the Bedouins live in extended families. The kids ran out to the vehicles waving and smiling. We threw them MRE's. We knew from experience around German towns that kids just love these things. God knows why, but I guess it's the neat packaging, and of course the candy. We were all suckers for smiles from those kids and when we saw them the MRE's flew.

After three days of running around we made it back to Henry. The word was passed down that the exercise, except for a few minor glitches, had gone extremely well. We got a feel for the formations, the commanders got a taste of how things were going to work, and we were able to see how the equipment would hold up. It seemed the tanks and other vehicles were doing extremely well; even better than expected. Commo, on the other hand .... let's just say business was about to heat up.

Chapter 12
Decisions

Sergeant T violently threw the 63 pound radio he was carrying to the sand floor of the tent. "How the fuck can we operate without a decent vehicle to transport this shit across the goddamn desert?" I looked at him and said nothing. I knew better.

It was the day after the exercise and we'd just been hit with 20 pieces of communications equipment needing repair by higher maintenance. The problems with dirt, sand, and constant use of radios were beginning to take their toll. The equipment was having a hard time keeping pace with the use it was getting. The dust and dirt, along with commanders leaving radios on 24 hours a day was wreaking havoc with the systems. It was an absolute imperative that the soldiers in my battalion could talk to one another. No one was gonna die because of a damn radio. They had to work. We started getting creative. Radios left on constantly and the coming hot days created excessive heat stress on the equipment. A wet towel on the top frame of the radio would alleviate some of that heat.

Sergeant T and I were overwhelmed. We had in excess of 160 radios in the battalion and 15% of them had gone down on the exercise. We'd given up the humvee, HQ-37, to battalion as soon as we'd arrive at the TAA. Sergeant T was mad as hell about it and had been mad every day since. Higher maintenance, the guys who ripped the guts out of the equipment after we'd identified the problem, was a ten kilometer drive through the desert. We'd been using deuce-and-a-half and five ton trucks to transport the radios across the rutted desert roads, but putting a radio in the back of one of those trucks was no different than throwing if off a building. We were getting equipment back from higher in worse shape than when it was sent.

I could see Sergeant T had cooled a bit, so I spoke. "I really don't know what the hell they think, Sarge. Somebody should get the idea that radios bouncing across the desert in a goddamn five ton is part of the reason they're having problems."

Transportation of radio equipment had not been high on the list of battalion priorities to this point. Sergeant Thompson was about to move it up a notch or two. The Red Lions were dead meat if no one was talking.

"Fuck it. I've had enough. I'm going to get the Major in on this, and if he doesn't listen the goddamn Colonel's gonna get an earful. This shit will stop."

Sergeant T was off to make another pitch to get us a vehicle. With 20 radios down in the battalion we had a good chance of finally being listened to .... It took four days, and in the meantime we commandeered Sergeant Burgess's hummer for transport, but it worked. We got a vehicle .... kind of.

Lines In The Sand

About that time, the 12th or 13th of February, Captain Hanks called the company to a meeting. He had that wide eyed look, the one he put on to let us think he was a little crazy. Events were moving quickly:

"Y'all better have your shit together now goddamnit, because if it ain't been together up to this point you've been lucky. There will be no room for fuckin' up where we're going .... That's right gentlemen, we're going to war." The CO was silent for a few seconds.

"What I'm going to tell you now is Secret gentlemen. It goes nowhere. Not in your letters back home, and sure as hell not in the phone calls some of your are getting to make." He stopped and looked at us a few seconds more. "On 16 February we move up here," he had a stick and was drawing formational lines in the sand, "FAA Butz. That's Forward Assembly Area Butz. At this particular place we will be 30 kilometers from the Iraqi border, just south of this designated neutral zone." He drew a diamond shaped box in the sand next to the line representing Iraq. "We will begin the move-out on the morning of the 16th, with our ETA being the evening of the 17th. It's a 100 kilometer march. Here is where we make last minute preparations. According to the latest information we move into this area," he pointed at southern Iraq on his makeshift map in the sand, and a real map the First Sergeant had laid out, "on 24 February. That's the day all hell breaks loose." His tone softened. "We're going to war gentleman and I want all of you to prepare yourselves. Some of you might need someone to talk to so the chaplain is here to listen. My job is to bring as many of you home from here as I can, but you have got to help me. I cannot bring all of you back if you're not thinking about what is going on around you. Keep your shit tight gentlemen! Don't piss me off and get yourself killed. All that paperwork and shit ...." He trailed off into silence. "Got that!"

A quiet, "Yes, Sir," went up amongst us.

"All right. That's all."

That evening, after the CO's speech, we were on our typical two hour stand-to, watching bombers fly overhead. Jets and bombers of all types had been flying over every night since our arrival in the desert. It seemed in these particular days, though, the numbers were increasing. Dog, soldier/sailor after his seagoing adventure, claimed to have counted over 50 jets on guard duty one night. I counted about 25 in the two hours of stand-to that evening. Dog also claimed to have seen the new F-117 stealth fighter go over one day. The planes we were seeing this evening were F-14's, F-16's, B-52's, and the like.

I was up in the hole with Evans, the kid from Indiana. Evans, at 18, was one of the youngest kids in the platoon. I knew the desert was wearing on him. It seemed that most of the older guys in the platoon were handling desert life better than the younger guys. The older guys, usually having a few tough experiences in their backgrounds, were able to keep things in perspective. Not that the desert wasn't hard on everybody's frame of mind. The wind and sand blowing constantly made people irritable. Add to that we had to look at the same faces day in and day out. We all had to think everyday about getting along with each other. The past few weeks I'd watched Evans' state of mind turn serious and very moody. The could-care-less attitude of youth had left.

About the first week after arriving at TAA Henry we were issued live ammunition. We carried six 30 round clips of M-16 ammo in the two carrying cases on our ammo belt, a 7th clip went in the weapon, if so ordered. The next day a young soldier from an armored unit attached to our brigade blew his brains out. The story went around that his wife had sent him a videotape of her fucking another man. She then asked for a divorce. He walked into the desert and stuck the M-16 into his mouth. The next day, after the suicide, the live ammo was taken from us and put in a central location at the platoon level. In the maintenance platoon we carried it in the tool truck. NCO's and officers still carried live on their person. Except for guard shifts and other designated times, the rest of us did not carry live ammo regularly.

Sitting in the hole watching the jets fly over that night, I wanted to tell Evans to get his shit together and stop being such a moody little prick, but I didn't. I remember him bitching about not having live ammo: "And what the hell are we suppose to do if some terrorist group comes over the hill?," he said .... I just listened.

Scout Dude

"Hey, Commo Dude, we got a bunch of new humvees and the LT sent me over to see if you guys can install radios in these things."

"Hey, Scout Dude," I said. "I hear you guys' Bradleys got delayed on some ship. You're gonna use humvees instead, ha?"

"Yeah. I think we can do our job better in the humvee than the Bradley anyway."

It was PFC Frank Bradish who came to get me that morning. Bradish was a scout with the Red Lions and the scouts were in a bind because their Bradley fighting vehicles were late in arriving to the desert. They had gotten hold of five or six humvees and if the Bradleys didn't arrive in time that's what they would use. I grabbed my tools and followed Bradish out to one of the hummers. The lieutenant in charge of the scouts had picked up radios from somewhere and had everything ready for me to install.

"Hey, Commo Dude, you think you can get this stuff working?"

"No problem, Scout Dude." Bradish always called me Commo Dude, so I started calling him Scout Dude. I liked the hell out of Bradish. Though I didn't work with the guy everyday, I worked on the scouts' radio equipment quite a bit and we'd run into each other when I was taking care of their radios. Bradish was a lanky, sandy haired kid with far-away, friendly eyes. I figured he was from California or something because he always referred to people as dudes. I found out later he was from Idaho. Bradish and I were talking about the radios and anything else other than the cold, rainy weather that day.

"You know, I think the army should change all the job titles they use," he said. "Instead of like, 94 Bravo, Medical Specialist, or whatever, it'd just be Medic Dude. Instead of your job .... What's your MOS, dude?"

MOS is Military Occupational Specialty. "I'm a 31 Victor, Unit Level Communications Maintainer."

"Yeah. It would be a lot simpler to just call it Commo Dude, and me just Scout Dude."

"Makes a lot of sense to me. Think how much simpler all the paperwork would be. Maybe you should submit that to one of those army suggestion programs."

"Hey, that's a good idea, dude. The army pays you if they use one of your suggestions?"

"You bet," I said.

"You're all right, Commo Dude."

"Thanks, Scout Dude."

The Scouts' Bradley fighting vehicles showed up in time before we moved out. The job that lay ahead for the scout platoon was full of danger. They are, like in the days of the cavalry scout, way out in front. They let the rest of us know what's up there. The scout platoon in the Red Lions was a bunch of guys who literally stepped to the beat of a different drummer; aware of their long tradition in the US army. Even in todays modern, technical army, the scout is still the trailblazer.

Oil Spill

It was around the day we were given the plans for our attack into Iraq that Saddam Hussein opened an oil pipeline which began spewing millions of barrels of oil into the Persian Gulf. We were getting news from US Armed Forces Radio, which was broadcasting from the Saudi military city of KKMC about 30 miles from us. For two days the oil poured into the Gulf. Finally a precision bombing raid closed off the oil, but not before the greatest oil spill in history had occurred. The spill had no military merit, as an amphibious assault is not hindered by oil. I thought about the beautiful waters of the Gulf and the huge schools of fish we'd seen and that now all of them would be dead. It pissed me off. It was time for a Saddam wake-up call and we were ready.

Wanton destruction was beginning to envelop Kuwait as it became apparent Hussein would not be able to keep the country he had invaded. The countries 900 or so oil wells were said to be rigged for destruction next.

For three days after the CO's speech we loaded vehicles and prepared for war. We had to have essential things for battle, but on the other hand there was a whole lot of unnecessary equipment that just made it harder for us to move. We began to lighten the load. We had huge semi-trailer units called connexes that were in a central brigade location; basically in the middle of nowhere. Most of the valuable things we had brought with us were loaded in those trailers. I remember loading a large air pump, sleeping cots, camouflage netting, and even a ping-pong table into the connexes. What the hell we needed a ping-pong table for, I had no idea. We buried and burned a lot of stuff we simply couldn't carry: old army tents too large and with too many holes; metal shelving used for storage we no longer needed. We lightened up considerably in three days time. On stand-to during those evenings I saw bonfires all around us as units in the area engaged in the same practice. There's a lot of junk buried for the Bedouins to dig up someday. We got word later that Bedouins had broken into the trailer connexes and stolen everything in them. Somewhere there's a desert family that's learned the game of ping-pong.

The Hummer

On the night of 15 February we lined up our vehicles for roll out to FAA Butz. We tore down the tents we'd been living in for the past three weeks and would sleep in our vehicles that night. I would be riding in the back of a deuce-and-a-half truck with Evans, Ronson, and a big tall Texan named Neiland. Going to war in the back of a truck was not an appealing thought. We had army cots laid out in which we'd lie on or sit during the trip. Evans said he'd bounced from the cot to the ceiling of the truck more than once on the way to TAA Henry from Dhahran. Not only would it be a rough ride, but dusty as hell, unless it rained constantly. I loaded my gear in the back of the truck and sacked out for the night.

The next morning was bright, sunny, and promised to be a warm day. I rolled out of the truck at sunrise and shaved my face, then brushed my teeth in cold Evian. I'd gotten used to shaving in cold water; I even liked it sometimes. The cold slap in the face from the Evian was a real eye-opener. Walking back to the deuce-and-a-half I saw everybody taking windows out of their vehicles and putting green army 100 mile-an-hour tape over all the headlights and taillights. The CO had given the order, which came from higher, saying the glare from windows could be seen for miles. About then tempers flew.

I'd gotten word that Sergeant Burgess wanted to see me, and about that same time Sergeant Smith (our other soldier/sailor from the overseas freighter trip) had given an order to a young specialist by the name of Gales to grab a couple of guys to hook up a trailer, or something of the like. Gales came around the corner of the deuce-and-a-half, pointed at me and Evans, "ordering" us to hook up the trailer. Well, to begin with that pissed me off. Because I was in a promotable to sergeant status I outranked him, even though we were both the same pay grade. I told him I was busy and to get somebody else.

Gales was a mechanic and mechanics work hard. Pulling engines and turning bolts is tough work. Commo guys, on the other hand, don't do the hard labor mechanics sometimes do. It occasionally created friction between me and the rest of the mechanics that was never expressed, but was there never-the-less. After I blew off his less than heedable order Gales accused me of being less than a hard worker; lazy as he put it. That really pissed me off. I've learned that the art of giving an order has a lot to do with tact. Since Gales needed my help, and he knew I outranked him, he should have used a different approach. Gales had only been in the service a little more than a year and had distinguished himself as a good soldier. He'd been promoted very quickly, some thought too quickly. I gave him what he deserved.

"Some no time in grade E-4 is going to tell me I'm lazy? I've been doing this shit for three and a half years and some no time in grade punk calls me lazy? After you've been through the schools and the shit I've been through in the army, then maybe you can call me lazy!" I turned and headed toward Sergeant Burgess' hummer as previously ordered. As I turned I saw Sergeant Smith chuckling. He'd watched the whole thing. I guess I'd learned the sergeant's art of "tearing somebody a new asshole".

By the time I'd gotten to see Sergeant Burgess he'd already heard about the argument. It's amazing how fast word travels in the army.

"What was that between you and Gales?"

"It's settled Sarge. Won't be no more problems."

"We're going to war here, 'J'. We got to work together."

"Yes, Sergeant." I liked the hell out of Sergeant Burgess. It seemed he had a rare gift. He was fair, tough, and knew about everything going on around him. His vast army experience made us respect him unquestionably. He looked at me with a very slight grin; ruddy cheeks and wizened eyes. There was always humor just under the surface when he eyeballed you.

"Here's your combat medic kit." He handed me a brand new green bag, about the size of a small backpack. In it were two IV's, bandages of all kinds, atropine injectors for nerve gas poisoning, and one other item; a full, very large injector of Valium The Valium was the antidote to the atropine nerve gas antidote. Atropine is a massive amphetamine designed to open a person up and stop, or flush through, the nerve agent. If someone's heart was about to explode from too much atropine, which was very possible, we were to shoot 'em up with the Valium These drugs were all in liquid form and encased in auto injector syringes. We simply had to slam them hard into a soldiers thigh area, through the clothing.

I'd taken the combat medic course before leaving for the Gulf. There were two or three of us in every platoon. I'd learned to give IV's, general first-aid, and CPR. We were the first line of aid before the company medics arrived. It was a good class; good stuff to know. We were also given one other pill that day. We were told the pill was for biological warfare; an anthrax antidote. The order to take this pill could only come from the division commander. We weren't told this, but I knew this was the experimental drug I'd heard about. I threw it in my medic bag.

"You want to drive a hummer there, 'J'?" I looked up at Sergeant Burgess as I rummaged through the bag.

"You don't even have to ask a question like that, Sarge. Where'd you get a hummer?"

"It's this air force humvee that's been sitting around the maintenance area waiting for a new front end since we got here. It's one that the air force boys drove over a cliff."

"You mean you got the parts in to fix it."

"Ahh, not exactly," Sergeant Burgess said that while eyeballing me humorously, making me a little uneasy. "The air force boys bent the wheels straight out to the sides when they went over the cliff. We heated the torsion bars underneath and just bent them back to normal."

"Can you drive the damn thing?"

"Oh, sure. I drove it over here. Seems to be fine. Don't drive it too fast over those bumps out there, that's all. Thing is, if those bars give underneath there could be a pretty quick stop, if you know what I mean."

"What do you mean, quick stop," I asked.

"Ha-ho-ho," Sergeant Burgess laughed. "Don't go faster than 35. Don't want those bars to give. You want to drive it or not?"

I walked back to the deuce-and-a-half, got my gear, and threw it into the humvee. I needed a TC (vehicle commander in army jargon, but just a second rider in this case) so I asked Neiland if he wanted to TC the vehicle: "It's a whole lot better' n ridin' in the back a this deuce-and-a-half," he said in his clear Texas drawl.

So Neiland and I loaded up the hummer and started taking out the windows and covering up the headlights, as per the CO's orders. After a visual check of the hummer, everything seemed fine. It seemed that by some round about way Sergeant T's pleas for a humvee had gotten through; as long as the wheels on the thing continued to point straight ahead, that is.

Chapter 13
FAA Butz

We left the cozy confines of Tactical Assembly Area Henry and headed for the wide open desert and a place designated Forward Assembly Area Butz. The designations forward and tactical assembly area are self explanatory; forward means way up there. As Neiland and I jumped into the hummer and popped it into drive I had my fingers crossed. Sergeant Burgess put a tow truck right behind us as we rolled out just in case everything went to hell with this vehicle. Everyone in maintenance knew about this hummer and more than a few expressed their doubts it would make it more than a few miles. Some said it was dangerous to even drive the thing. A snapped torsion bar at 40 or 50 miles per hour down the highway is a dangerous thing. I thought about the risk and figured I wasn't going to be driving down a highway anyway. 35 miles per hour is as fast as it gets across a rutted desert. It did cross my mind that the front end could go in the middle of a battle. That was a very bad thought, so I forgot about it. Sergeant T had fought and fought for a hummer; maybe we had one.

We made it a mile; then two. Pretty soon we were rolling along taking the bumps as well as any other vehicle. Sergeant Burgess and his troop did a hell of a job on that hummer. Driving through the desert beats the hell out of a vehicle and we couldn't always play it safe by going slow over the bumps.

Neiland was a good choice to have with me. He was a strong, tall kid with the damndest Texas drawl I'd ever heard. Neiland was the hardest working soldier in the platoon. He had a farm boy attitude and outlook that made any job given him one he could accomplish, given a little hard work. He also wasn't a bad mechanic. If we got stranded I figured Neiland could get us out of it.

After leaving the assembly area we drove to a staging area a few klicks into the desert. We would travel to the forward assembly area in battle configuration with the rest of the brigade. As we pulled into our places at the center of the huge V that held the brigade support vehicles, I looked out over a sea of military hardware. Vehicles stretched to the horizon. On my right I had Chaparral missile systems with Vulcan machine gun crews. These were air defense specialist's, there to protect our 1000 vehicle convoy. The convoy included semi-truck fuelers, water trucks, troop trucks, ammunition trucks, medics, mechanics, and communications. All that support, and more, just to keep one brigade in an armored division working.

I had been told that my brigade, 1st of the 3rd Armored Division, was the heaviest brigade in the US army. I had no doubt about that as I looked out over it. Wrapped all around our support convoy were the main elements of the brigade. These were two armored battalions, of which the Red Lions were one; two armored cavalry battalions, and an artillery battalion. Each armored battalion consisted of 58 M1A1 Abrams main battle tanks, a scout platoon with six Bradley fighting vehicles, a mortar platoon with four M-113 mobile launching vehicles, and another shitload of support vehicles that traveled directly in its rear. Each armored cavalry battalion had a mix of M1A1 tanks and Bradley's totaling roughly 70 combat vehicles; the artillery battalion contained the 155 mm self propelled howitzer with a range of roughly 23 miles. I find it difficult to describe the scale of what I was looking at that day. I can only say that on flat ground I looked from horizon to horizon and saw nothing but military hardware. It seemed I could jump from vehicle to vehicle for as far as I could see and never hit the ground .... I tied a green medical sling bandage from my medic bag over my nose and mouth like a bandana. I was about to experience a dust storm like no other; a corps size man made one. I threw on a pair of goggles and we were off.

Contemplations

The radio had reported earlier this day that Saddam wanted to withdraw from Kuwait, if certain demands were met (later George Bush would call this the cruel hoax). As we waited in line getting ready to roll out I remember a few people yelling at the sound of this news. Sergeant T, in a vehicle just ahead of us, yelled, "Don't bet on it!" For just a minute I felt that maybe Saddam Insane had realized what was about to happen to him and we wouldn't be going through with this thing. The feeling only lasted a minute, though. As all those vehicles started to move out I knew there was little going to stop it. The commitment of personnel and material had been made. The machine was in gear and would do battle. The 24th was eight days away.

As I realized war with Iraq was really going to happen, my feelings would best be described as complicated. On the one hand I hated life in the desert. I can describe over and over the sandstorms, the cold and wet climate at that time, the bad food and tedious hours on guard duty. It was a damn hard way to live. I wanted the thing to get going and then be over. On the other hand, fear, the unknown, was real too.

I knew that I had little or no control over events that were going to happen. As things started to unfold it was comforting, in a way, to know that I could do little to affect them. My only control was over the things that I had to do in my day to day life; drive a humvee and fix radios. I could not control the decisions of politicians and generals. If I could not affect these decisions, then, I could see little reason to think, or even worry much, about what could happen. I was simply a cog in a wheel that was now in motion.

For the better part of a year and a half I'd been reading different books on personal fulfillment, spirituality of a sort. Reading this type of material helped me deal with the difficult times associated with army life. It is hard to explain, but it seems I'd reaffirmed my spiritual beliefs just for this particular event. I had simply come to realize, without doubt, that there was more, much more, than this life we live day to day.

I was raised in the Catholic Church and as I grew older I began to see the Church as a relic; something old which held little meaning for me. In a modern scientific world, did not the answer to life lie in science? With our new science, then, where is there room for faith? Isn't the question of life and death answered by DNA? Of course, something inside told me DNA isn't all there is. It seemed I knew this, but I needed it explained in terms I could relate to; modern terms. The answers I learned are little different than what the Church has always taught. The reaffirmation of my faith is something I'll call pure knowledge. The Church has told us to have faith when we doubted. I never need to have doubted.

Tap Line and Beyond

Even though the trip to the forward area was only 70 miles or so, it was slow going; about 20 miles per hour tops as we negotiated the rough desert terrain. We had to cross back over Tap Line Road and the huge oil pipeline that skirted it. The pipeline was above ground where we crossed so getting around it with an army was a problem. The answer was to go over it. The pipeline itself was about two or three meters in diameter and suspended some three to five meters off

115

the desert floor. Army engineers simply built a dirt road over top of the line and we drove over.

We arrived at the FAA that evening. We assembled for the night in a tactical circular formation with each company having its own formation. It reminded me of a wagon-train circle from the old West. It served the same purpose as in those days; all sides would be covered. Neiland and I slept in the front seats of the hummer that night. We got as comfortable as possible in the cramped seats (I'd learned to sleep in any contorted position if I was tired enough). The next day we'd be moving to a more permanent site. We awoke the next morning to dark clouds and as we began moving forward a downpour began. With no windows in the hummer, driving was a bitch. Another hummer had gone by us with MRE container boxes cut out to fit over the windshield. We caught on fast. Neiland grabbed two MRE boxes, cut small holes for forward vision, then with the trusty green 100 mile-an-hour tape fit them over the windshield. With all my rain gear, goggles, and boots, I was still soaked.

We didn't have far to drive. First Sergeant Dillon directed us into our circular formation. As soon as we were parked the rain stopped. I figured it was good training; driving in a downpour with no windows. After the vehicles were set up in our company area we received the order to dig in. Unlike the desert where we had come from 70 miles to our south, this area was perfectly flat and desolate. There was no natural cover of hills or sand dunes here, only open space. I grabbed a shovel and my entrenching tool, heading for the front of the line of vehicles. We dug four man foxholes 10 meters in front of each vehicle. Cook, Sergeant Smith, myself, and Dudley dug a hole in front of the tool truck.

Dudley was talking about that number jillion. "Hey 'J', tell us just how many fishes we seen that day."

Late Night Thunder

As soon as we finished digging in we got our personal setups in order. Since we were on the move, most of the soldiers were sleeping in their vehicles. There was not enough room in the hummer for both Neiland and myself, so we grabbed our handy rain ponchos and each of us built ourselves a little hooch. With three tent stakes for support at the bottom end, and the vehicle to tie to on the top end, we were able to make a shelter that sloped at a 45 degree angle from each side of the vehicle to the ground. Each was just high and long enough to slip a cot underneath. It would keep the rain off.

FAA Butz was about 30 kilometers from the Iraqi border. Jets flew over in great numbers day and night. Flashes of light from the bombing campaign in Kuwait and the southwestern corner of Iraq spilled into the night sky. Occasional shows from fighter jets as they flew over at very low altitudes highlighted these waiting days.

About three or four days after our arrival at Butz, asleep at night in my hooch alongside the hummer, I awoke to a deafening roar. I bolted up looking at my watch. It was about 0230. A jet had come in low over the top of our area. From the sound it had banked straight up over our company circle. I threw my feet over the side of the cot and waited for the bombs to hit. I knew Iraqi jets could reach us easily here. Nothing happened; the jet faded into the distance.

The next day Sergeant T and I were eating lunch and talking about the loud fuckin' jet that had woke up the whole camp last night: "I was over to higher maintenance this morning and the lieutenant in charge of those Chaparral missiles was there," Sergeant T said. "I found out what his job was and asked him about that jet flying over us the middle of last night. He started going off about that shit. Said they

117

were all scared as hell because they couldn't identify him as friendly or enemy, something about his transponder IFF code not being turned on. They locked on to that old boy."

"Well, it scared the b'Jesus out of me last night. I thought, man, here we go. They found us."

"I think everybody was shittin'. This lieutenant said his missiles were locked on and following him right in. The jet knew he was locked on to and pulled straight up over the camp. I guess the computer locks the missiles to automatically fire. Then the jet turned on its transponder, or whatever. The LT said he had to reach over to push a button, otherwise that jet was about three seconds from being bye-bye."

After the shock of being awoke in the middle of the night by a screaming jet, the remaining few days at FAA Butz were pretty tame. On the 22nd a Scud alert was called. With the wide open space of the desert there was little we could do except stay away from the vehicles. It went south toward KKMC and was hit by a Patriot we were told. We heard constant bombing from the border area, though we were under no attack of any kind. I later learned Hussein never knew we were in this area. With his radar and communications crippled by the bombing campaign he had little idea of our location. The end-around plan, going north in a long sweeping move through Iraq, instead of directly at his dug-in troops in Kuwait, was a brilliant plan. Why go directly at divisions when a long border exists with few troops to guard it? In looking at a map it's pretty easy to see this makes perfect sense. Sergeant T and I talked about this strategy well before we knew it would be used, proving, of course, that two lowly commo pukes had had the same grasp of military tactics as a four star general. I don't think we were getting paid enough ....

About 23 February, Sergeant T was told by battalion HQ to use the air force humvee for a commo vehicle. Finally we had a hummer! Since this vehicle was "technically" not repaired (the parts to fix it hadn't arrived), we couldn't "technically" give it back to the air force. Since we were in need of vehicles anyway, this "technical" solution worked out great. The air force boys attached to our unit asked about the vehicle occasionally. Our answer to them was that it just wasn't fixed. When they asked why it was being driven around we told them it was being test driven, or something of the like.

As supply lines began to stretch, spare parts were getting hard to come by. The air force hummer was considered an extra in the battalion, so when the Major's vehicle had a starter go out guess where a good starter was found? In the mornings I had to crank the thing over ten or more times until the starter became warm enough to catch and turn the engine. We could put up with the starter since after it was warm the thing would always work fine. Believe me, though, when it came to priority we were dead last on the totem pole. The medics lieutenant had a bad generator in his humvee so the day before we were to roll into Iraq the decision was made to pull our generator and give it to the medics. Now we had a bad generator! The hummer was a diesel; it needed no spark plugs. As long as the vehicle was running we were fine, we just wouldn't shut it off! I had few worries about bullets or artillery shells. I knew the thing that might get Sergeant T and I dead quicker than anything was getting stranded in the desert. Parts or no parts, the broken down air force hummer had to get us through. I would will the son-of-a-bitch to make it.

February 24, 1991

Dear Family,

Well, as I write this we are about to leave for the border. We have been about 30 miles from Iraq for the last week. Have been able to hear the bombing at night, but have come under no fire here. A scud scare two days ago, but it traveled south of us and a Patriot nailed it.

We have 2nd Armored Cavalry Regiment and 1st Infantry Division in front us as we are the last division to go in at our side of the crossing. We watched the diplomatic efforts with interest, but we were always skeptical. I heard last night 190 oil rigs were ablaze and with him systematically blowing up rigs, talk of a pullout is just talk ....

With the divisions in front of us, who are already in, it is possible we will never even load weapons. If our front line troops see action we in support areas should not see anything. If we have to fight at my level shit has gone to hell. This I do not expect ....

We are lining up to roll. I guess I'll give you the play by play as I don't know when I'll be able to send this. It's drizzling today, but clear in the distance. Sure is more rain here than I ever expected. Got to go.

Love

The day had finally come. 24 February, 1991. Sergeant T and I packed the hummer with tools, personal gear, boxes of MRE's, and cases of bottled water.

At 0900 hours we lined up in brigade formation. I had slaved (jump started) the hummer to get it going and we were sitting at idle. About 1100 hours we began to roll toward the border. We stopped often as we were awaiting other units at our front to cross in. About 1400 hours we stopped and went to MOPP level 2. A chemical attack was expected and we were told to take a pill. We would take the little white nerve agent antidote pills every eight hours from now on. An hour later my insides were in an upheaval.

In the history of the Red Lion battalion it reads: "We crossed the Saudi-Iraqi border at 1621 hours, 24 February, 1991." We were some distance behind the lead elements. It was a 15 foot high wall of sand that marked the border. A trail just wide enough for a tank had been cut through the middle of the wall. About 1645 hours Sergeant T and I drove that air force hummer into Saddam Hussein's Iraq.

Technodevastation outside Basra, Iraq.

The view from the tent at our encampment in Northern Kuwait.

Headquarters Company commo: Sergeant Milano on the left, myself, and Sergeant T.

The broken down air force hummer, Sergeant T and a Specialist Galbreath from Bravo Company commo. The dark sky is oil smoke haze from the fires.

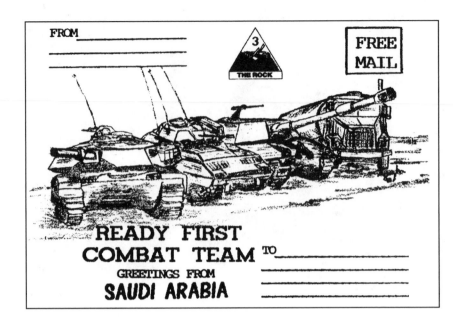

Safwan.

*Half an hour after the ceasefire; myself kneeling,
Ronson at right, Gales left.*

A blown T-55 Iraqi tank.

In the pumphouse with the Jordanian munitions on the day I traveled with Sergeant Wills.

Charlie company of the Red Lions.

The Iraqi town of Safwan after the war.

The child in the pretty flowered dress in Safwan.

Dudley, with his hands up, Cook, the artist, on the right.

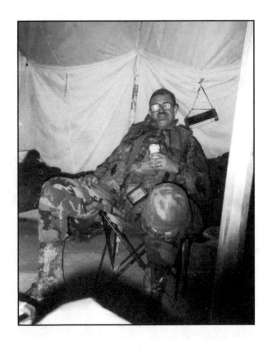

Sergeant T!

Chapter 14
War

An eerie twilight descended from a darkened sky as we drove. We were in a hostile country, a country we were at war with. I expected some kind of resistance: troops, artillery, enemy tanks; there were none. We simply drove in. It was hard to believe. I couldn't get over the brashness of plowing a hole through the border and just driving in. Since it was getting dark it was hard to get a good look at this country we had just invaded, not that I expected this desert to be any different than the desert I had just left.

We traveled slowly that evening, stopping often. There was a northerly wind blowing, but not extremely hard. I could see flashes of light to our south. It could have been from the noise of the convoy, or the wind blowing from the opposite direction, but there was no sound from those flashes. Something was happening there. I expected artillery rounds to come in any time, but it didn't happen.

We stopped at 2000 hours, or thereabouts, arranging our vehicles in the familiar circle formation. Since we couldn't restart the hummer without slaving it from another vehicle it sat at idle all night, the diesel engine purring continuously. With no windows there was no worry about asphyxiation. We tried to park away from the wind, but it still came in the open front of the vehicle. I left the heater running, keeping us somewhat comfortable. A guard list came around and I had the shift from 0100 to 0200 hours. Sergeant T was in the passenger seat smoking a Winston. "What'd you think of this shit?"

"Seems pretty quiet so far," I said.

"Too damn quiet."

It was quiet. Maybe the hummer idling was drowning those flashes of light to our south, I expected some kind of noise from that at least. I tuned my Walkman to a static filled BBC news report. I could get some English language news reports, though most of the AM and FM bands contained news in Arabic or other languages I couldn't understand. Over 200 oil wells were reported on fire; scorched earth policy; destroy it if you can't have it. I fell off to sleep slumped in the front seat of the hummer.

About 0050 hours I awoke for my guard shift. The previous guard handed me ammunition for my M-16. We still were not carrying live ammo regularly on our persons. One thing I remember from infantry tactics training at the NCO Academy is how often we killed each other; friendly fire it's called. In a 1000 vehicle convoy if every-one had ammo and we were attacked there'd be a lot of dead friendlies. In the tight knit way in which this convoy traveled we'd most likely be shooting the shit out of each other. There was plenty of ammunition around as it was. .50 caliber machine guns were mounted atop deuce-and-a-half trucks on the outside lanes of the convoy. Small arms ammunition for the maintenance platoon was in the tool truck, which I kept in sight as we drove. We had live ammunition on guard duty, but didn't load up, we carried it. The white flashes of light still blinked in the pitch black southern sky. The wind cut through me making little swirls of blowing sand, always finding my open eyes. At least the rain had held off.

It was before first light when I was rousted for good from my crumpled position in the front seat bed of the hummer. I put on my combat boots, then the chemical overboots, and rolled up my sleeping bag. I still was making it a point to shave every day, cold water or not. In past experience I'd use humvee side mirrors for shaving, but because of possible glare, as with the windows, we'd taken them all off, so I'd learned to shave without a mirror. Breakfast that morning was a cold MRE and a pill. The little white nerve agent antidote pills were turning my insides real well. I made sure I had time to grab our makeshift outhouse chair and take a walk in the desert to relieve some of that churning. The chair we had was a real winner. The mechanics blow torched a nice round hole in the middle of a steel folding chair. Dig a hole in the desert, set the chair over top, take a Stars and Stripes newspaper along, and relax. Enjoy the wide open spaces.

After a breakfast of cold spaghetti and applesauce we fueled up the hummer. I calculated that we'd burned only four gallons of diesel idling all night. We did shut it down for a while to check the oil and other fluids. I had another vehicle there to slave from right away. Keeping the damn thing running was my top priority. We pulled out mid-morning, 25 February.

It drizzled on and off all day. The only thing good about the rain was that there was no dust. During the periods it wasn't raining I was amazed at how fast the dust formed. It could be dry for just a few hours and the dust would be rolling. We drove all day. Our hummer was at about the mid-point of the brigade support elements (the 1000 vehicles). Bradley's and air defense missiles were to our sides. We didn't stop for lunch, chowing MRE's as we drove. Everyone was doing the same as MRE boxes and empty containers of bottled water littered our path. We were trashing the Iraqi desert. In Saudi we were told not to litter the desert, but in Iraq this order seemed to have been forgotten. Maybe it was a statement to Saddam; leave a trail and dare him to find us.

All through this day of the 25th we met no resistance. We were making an incredible number of miles and seeing absolutely nothing; barren, lifeless nothing. I expected at least to see Bedouin camps or stray camels, but none were to be found. We'd traveled all through various parts of the Saudi desert, but this was the most barren I had ever seen. The word was we were straddling the Kuwaiti border to our south, but I wasn't sure how many miles away it was. Captain Hanks had later given the figure 22 miles, but maps from the first couple of days travel showed us to be much farther from Kuwait. We drove through the mud, and then the dust, all day. We stopped occasionally as commanders figured where to lead us. Apache and Cobra attack choppers straddled our sides, frequently flying directly over our formations. We drove on, smoking cigarettes, drinking bottled water, and chowing MRE's.

EPW's

By early evening of the 25th we were 70 miles into Iraq. Sergeant T went to a platoon sergeant's briefing and came back with word that the scouts had picked up 25 or 30 EPW's (Enemy Prisoners of War). Talk was that they were literally starving to death. In return for food and water they had given any information we wanted of them. Even the highest ranking officers were supposedly telling all. At the sight of us they had lifted their AK-47 rifles over their heads and immediately surrendered.

"I guess they ate those MRE's like there was no tomorrow."

"Jesus, they must have been goddamned hungry." I was finishing the last of an oatmeal cookie bar. How the hell anyone could make an oatmeal cookie taste that lifeless was beyond me.

"They're starving to death, I guess. The scouts were saying one guy they picked up was from Chicago!"

"Chicago! Nooo. They must have been bullshitting."

"Nope, it's true. They picked this guy up and he started speaking perfect English. The scouts asked him how he knew English so well and he said 'I'm from fuckin' Chicago!'"

"No shit?"

"No shit." Sergeant T laughed and I was laughing. "Yeah, the guy is some professor, came to Iraq to visit family or something, they grabbed his ass and put him in the army!"

"Unbelievable! They must be really hurting for men?"

"Looks like it. These guys were just stragglers today, some of them deserted because they had no food. The big boys, the Republican Guard, are up there. We're headed right at 'em."

As darkness approached the booming of artillery started to our south. It was a few explosions at first and then became a barrage. Constant thunder rattled and cracked through the evening air. It hadn't rained hard that day, occasional drizzles, but the damp air had to have carried that sound a hell of a distance. It sounded maybe 20 or 30 klicks to our south. Sergeant T said we would be staying put for the night. The spot we were in wasn't much, right in the middle of no-where. Our vehicles were stopped in place, in line. We didn't make the typical circle formation this evening. We would be ready to go on a moments notice if need be.

We decided to make ourselves comfortable. In a brainstorm Sergeant Thompson decided to sleep on the hood of the vehicle. The air force had left a small tent in the rear of the hummer so we unrolled it, draped it over the hood of the hummer, and tied it off at the top and front grill of the vehicle. It made a nice little niche on the hood. Sergeant T crawled through the open windows, layed out his bag and slept right there. I was able to lay out my gear along the two front seats where at least I could stretch out. It wasn't bad, especially with a war raging around us.

We decided to shut the hummer down this night since the tool truck was right next to us for a quick slave. I slipped out of my chemical overboots and my regular boots, leaving the charcoal suit overgarments on. There was chemical detection paper all over the hummer and I had watched this stuff all day as we drove. It turns a red or yellow color if it detects a certain chemical agent in the air. I thought about chemical shit all the time. I rationalized my fear, figuring the front lines would get hit first giving us time in the rear to prepare. In reality, though, chemical artillery shells would reach us in the rear formations easily. The support elements were good targets for chemical. We didn't have the purification systems that exist inside M-1 tanks. I had my hand around my gas mask as I crawled into my bag. The explosions from the south seemed to be increasing. As darkness came the flashes from those explosions lit the southern sky. The thundering surrealness of it crashed like waves around the hummer. The noise of this thundering battle enveloped us all night, unceasingly, waking me many times.

February 26, 1991
Dear Family,

We are in Iraq. We crossed the border the evening of the 24th. Everyone we meet simply throws their hands up. I would too. We have a 300 mile wide column moving through this country. You cannot believe the number of vehicles. It is unpicturable as the scope is so massive.

I hear that Saddam told his troops to move back behind the border to his August 1 position. That is exactly where we are going. I am unclear as to what our mission is then. Obviously things are going extremely well and right to plan. We are still shelling their positions in Kuwait as I heard constant artillery bombardment all night long to our south. He obviously hasn't moved yet. I would say he should soon as there will be very quickly nothing left.

It is early in the morning (about 7 o'clock). The shelling and rocketing has started again to our south. Deep base thunder. Multiple launch rocket systems and howitzer. I can hardly imagine the devastation of multiple launch rockets. We are rolling, will write later.

Love,

After our early start on the morning of the 26th, we moved haltingly all day. It was our third straight day of travel and so far this day was a copy of the other two. Sergeant T in the passenger seat chainsmoking Winstons, me driving, constantly reminding myself to stay in the tracks. There were land mines that were either here or soon would be at positions to our front. Low clouds with intermittent rain and drizzle continued most of the day.

Since we were moving constantly, it was also our third straight day of MRE diet. When we were in one spot for a while the cooks could set up and break the monotony a little. With the steady diet of MRE's and the nerve gas antidote pills, my guts continued their steady churning.

Hussein's Republican Guard was directly in the path we were on and we knew it. During our stops this day the firing to our south kept up. Apache and Cobra helicopter gunships flew back and forth along our sides constantly. A slow incremental increase in activity continued throughout the day. Though we moved haltingly, when we did move we drove fast; 30 and 40 miles per hour bouncing across the desert. This made me worry about the beat up hummer, but it had so far carried us well.

To this point we had had little problem with commo. Sergeant Milano had been assigned to battalion headquarters and was appeasing those guys as best he could. Battalion HQ was no easy task for a commo man. Officers wanted perfect commo at all times, but the airwaves are not always a perfect means of communication. At this point, even if radios started going down, they would not be fixed. Higher support teams were moving as much as we were and had no time for repairs. We could do a lot of repairs on the spot, but major repairs of the radios were done by higher. From now on the equipment had to function.

We traveled another 30 miles that day. By early evening we were over 100 miles into Iraq. We had been stopped for some time in a nondescript part of the desert. The topography here was the same as everywhere else we'd been in Iraq; flat and lifeless. I was walking around the hummer, staring at the mass of steel and metal vehicles surrounding me as far as I could see. It was evening chow time and I was in the process of finishing up. I suppose I had lit a cigarette because I was leaning on the hood of the hummer having a conversation with one of the mechanics, Evans or maybe Neiland, and it started.

It was just a swoosh to the north side of our convoy. A bright light leaving the earth at great speed, and then another, and another, and another. The multiple launch rocket batteries straddling our sides had begun their assault. Two batteries were firing to our north, and then another began to our front. The rockets are fired in a series of twelve. As they are launched from their tubes I could see a slight delay until the rocket propulsion catches hold and thrusts them lightning quick into the atmosphere. The targets were to our easterly facing front, with the rockets flying over forward elements of the convoy. Sometimes a whole series of twelve rockets were let go at once; twelve white fiery flames shooting into the atmosphere; enough firepower to eliminate anything that moved in a 1000 by 1000 meter grid square. The firing started at 1900 hours to the best of my recollection. I watched it go on all evening and into the early morning hours. The 155 mm howitzer fire started to our front soon after. The booming fire to our south I had heard all day had now turned into our own firing. The only difference now was that the flashes of light matched the booms, and it was a hell of a lot louder.

We watched in awe the most incredible fireworks I'm sure any of us had ever seen. Deadly fireworks I knew. The Iraqis would later call it the "steel rain." As the rockets close in on their targets they open up, delivering thousands of tiny bomblets which drop like "rain" on opposing forces. There were some eight divisions of Guard troops to our front as we hit them with our corps size element. The "steel rain" fell incessantly on those divisions all that night.

At about 2000 hours that same night, word came over to the hummer that Sergeant Burgess wanted a platoon meeting. I grabbed my weapon and headed for the tool truck, the usual center for our maintenance platoon. Sergeant Burgess had a mean, bad look on his face as we approached the tool truck. I knew this would be no fun; the old Sarge got worked up only occasionally. He started to speak; his expression eerie, painful:

"HQ-26...." He started in a halting voice. "Scout platoon Bradley, HQ-26, was hit with Iraqi T-72 machine gun and main gun rounds." There were 20 men from maintenance standing around him and he managed to look each of us dead in the eye. "Staff Sergeant Stephans and Private First Class Stokes are dead." He pronounced dead with a quick finality that made my face burn. "Private First Class Bradish looks like he'll lose a leg." Scout Dude. My friend. The burning in my face spread. "Sergeant Goodman has a sunken chest wound." His voice raised a whole octave. "If you haven't figured it out yet this shit is fucking real gentlemen! I want you to think about your friends who are dead, and hurt, real hard! His voice softened. "You will pay attention to what is going on around you .... That's all." His last sentence was just a whisper.

We walked away in silence. The rocketing, which I hadn't noticed for some time, again invaded my senses, continuing its merciless assault at our flank.

Chapter 15
Tawakalna

February 27, 1991

Dear Family,

We are about 100 miles into Iraq. We made contact with his Republican Guard last night. The battle is still occurring. Rocket fire and artillery all night and today. We lost two scouts from my company last night as they got too close. I knew these guys and it put a lump in my throat.

The news reports from Kuwait say it is all but over there. 100,000 EPW's this morning. The Guard here in Iraq is a different story as these are his best. Schwarzkopf said we will take down the Guard here, whether they run, hide, or fight, and that is occurring presently.

I have a feeling when this battle is finished our job is not complete. I believe they are thinking of taking his government out of power, though, no one has said this yet. I believe we are going to Baghdad. I do not know if this will occur or not. We'll see ....

Love

Carey

We stayed in our positions the whole night of the 26th. We watched as the rocket and artillery barrage dropped tons of steel on the Republican Guard divisions to our front. There were eight Guard divisions and my division, US 3rd Armored, attacked the division known as Tawakalna.

Other major units around us as part of VII Corps were: the US 2nd Armored Cavalry Regiment, which preceded us into Iraq and was ahead of us until the morning of the 26th. At that time we passed through them, attacking the Tawakalna on the night of the 26th; the British 1st Armored Division, which fought and destroyed 80 tanks according to news reports; the US 1st Armored Division; the US 2nd Armored Division; the US 1st Infantry Division (Mechanized); and the US 1st Cavalry Division (Armored). 100,000 troops and 1200 tanks made up VII Corps.

Haze

About mid-morning on the 27th we began to move. We traveled some 10 klicks and stopped. The bombardment began again. The general idea was to soften the areas at our front with a hell of an artillery barrage, then drive into those areas taking on directly the shell-shocked survivors.

As we drove that day I noticed a haze in the sky that didn't seem to be just from the clouds and drizzle we'd experienced these last four days. The cloudy haze was heavier, darker somehow; clouds dark enough to hold rain, but no rain falling. News reports claimed 600 oil wells were burning in Kuwait. I pointed out the haze to Sergeant T and told him I thought it was from oil smoke. He didn't believe that at first, saying we must have been a hell of a ways from those fires. We later found out the haze "was" smoke. In the weeks and months to come the smoke would cover tens of thousands of square miles.

The rainy weather, fog, and oil smoke haze were ideal conditions for us and our allies in the battle. With fog and haze hiding our approach, long range sights saw through it destroying enemy equipment at will. The superior technology of that sighting equipment gave the United States and its allies an edge which the Republican Guard and its Soviet built equipment could not begin to match. We were all surprised to learn the T-72 Soviet tank, the Guards most vaunted weapon, had half the sighting distance of our own M1A1 through haze and fog. This incredible allied advantage killed Republican Guard tanks before they could ever know what was happening. They never saw their enemy.

All that day we moved in spurts; helicopter gunships continually flew over our positions providing support and firepower to the battle at our front. I remember coming over a small hill to see huge steel cylinders, which had earlier carried multiple launch rockets, litter the desert. We moved in unison with the launchers as they stopped, fired their rockets, dumped the spent rocket-carrying cylinders and moved ahead.

News was filtering through to us of other events connected to the war. It was about this time the barracks in Dhahran were hit by a Scud missile. This was the same general area we had been in for three weeks during January. The Scud warhead had hit a warehouse in the MGM Grand area killing 28 and injuring many more. In a seven day period during my stay in Dhahran we had some five to seven Scud alerts, with multiple missiles into the area on any given alert. Eventually one had to land.

A company support unit with another division had been wiped out the day before because they had been left in the open without protection. 29 US troops were killed. Support units, like the one I traveled in, were called "soft targets." We had no armor on our vehicles for protection. Enemy tanks tear into soft targets with no mercy. Except for .50 caliber machine guns on trucks at our left and right flanks, we had little defense. We depended on those Bradley and M-1 guys to take care of us. Still, I kept the tool truck with the M-16 ammo in sight.

Stragglers

About mid-afternoon of the 27th we stopped in a large basin. A gradual slope stretched in front of us to the horizon. After we'd stopped the howitzers and MLRS began another barrage to our front. We were parked in the bottom of the basin, the whole of the 1st Brigade, 3rd Armored Division support unit stretched up the gradual slope to my front. We were told we'd be in this position for a few hours. Sergeant Thompson and I broke open a new box of MRE's, deciding to chow. We'd been eating on the move for three of the last four days so it was nice to be at a stand-still during chow. We were still religiously taking our nerve gas antidote pills. I wanted to stop taking them because my stomach was in such an uproar, but Sergeant T, like the good NCO he was, made damn sure we stayed on our eight hour schedule. We had been in MOPP 2 for three straight days. I was thanking God above that it hadn't been hot. The charcoal suit was great in the cool weather, but bulky. We were now coming into areas where previously the Guard had been located. There were Iraqi mines here as well as cluster bombs from the US multiple launch rockets. The territory was becoming decidedly more dangerous.

As evening approached I saw six or seven strange looking men walk from the front of the support vehicle formation to the rear. They passed about 50 meters from my position. They were dressed shabbily without a common uniform, had long hair, some had beards. I could see they were carrying two boxes of MRE's and a case of bottled water between them. I looked long and hard for about a minute, then it dawned on me they were EPW's. They were smiling and joking with guys on the outside lane of our convoy. What struck me as really odd, though, was that they walked freely to the rear without a guard. I later saw an abandoned PC as we moved out from this position. I figured they had just surrendered peacefully and the guys up front had given them MRE's and water, took their weapons, and told them to go to the rear where the MP's were set up. They seemed only too happy. Many, many Iraqi soldiers simply surrendered at the sight of us; mainly for food.

Minefield

As darkness descended on the 27th, the sky around us was lit with the fires and explosions of battle. Tanks from the Red Lions and other units in my brigade and division had been, engaging Guard troops for 24 hours at this point. Though I could hear the battle to our front, until now I had seen little except the rocket fire. We kept up, though, with the news and it was better than good. The Red Lions had taken hundreds of EPW's and had engaged and destroyed a number of enemy tanks. The roar and deep bass explosions went on furiously around us, intensified it seemed by the darkness. A massive red glow lit the horizon as flashes of lightning, or maybe artillery bursts, struck randomly along it.

We were given word we would be traveling this night. Sergeant T and I both had a set of night vision goggles, so we pulled them out of their cases and began adjusting them to our faces. There was no moon and this would be another decided advantage. The night vision equipment (which used stars or any other ambient light to intensify the nighttime) on the tanks and Bradleys had double the range of the Iraqi's here, too, giving the M1A1 and Bradley fighting vehicle complete and devastating supremacy for night battle.

About 2000 hours we began to roll. I strapped the goggles to my face, pulling the full harness used to support them over the top of my head. They fit snugly and I was able to put my Kevlar helmet on over the harness. I turned a switch one click and a two dimensional world of black and white outlines with a light green background greeted me. The technology of war had given me eyes in the dark. I inadvertently turned my goggles to the infrared position making anything that produces heat show up as a white brightness; the front end of vehicles show white from engine heat. This can be distracting and so could be clicked off to show normal outlines. Any light can blind a person for an instant if he or she wears the goggles in the infrared mode; a lit match is a complete white-out. We traveled in what is called black-out drive. Small lights are installed on the taillights and headlights of all military vehicles. They are subtle enough to be seen for only a short distance.

As we began to move I looked to my left and the infrared sighting on my goggles picked up a small, bright white ball on the sand. I figured it to be an anti-personnel mine, or possibly an unexploded bomblet left over from an MLRS hit, still hot from its drop some hours ago. About then a hell of an explosion with a bright white fireball hit about 500 meters to our front. "Artillery or a mine!," Sergeant T yelled through the growing roar around us. As we rolled up to the place where the round or whatever had hit, a five-ton truck was lying nose down with its wheels blown out to the sides. A small fire burned beneath it but looked mostly out as GI's with halon fire extinguishers surrounded the truck. As the vehicles to my front cut a new path around the blown five-ton, Sergeant T and I got a good look at the damage as we drove by. The driver's cab was intact so it looked as if no one had been injured. We had, unbelievably, taken no enemy artillery to this point and it didn't seem that now was the time it would start. "If it was an anti-tank mine it seems it'd blown more of the vehicle!" Sergeant T yelled.

"Maybe it was just personnel!" I yelled back.

"Maybe!"

The two dimensional world of the goggles had altered the picture my brain was receiving. It seemed no different than seeing something on a movie screen; flat, distant. The feeling of reality was diminished. Only reason told me what I was seeing was reality. I looked over at Sergeant T as he pulled a rain poncho over his head and lit a Winston.

"Look at that shit, Sarge!" Sergeant T lifted his head from under the rain poncho after dragging on his smoke. Coming to the top of the low hill that lay at our front all that afternoon, the battle lay before us. A long low basin stretched into the distance with burning vehicles smoldering at innumerable places. In my night vision goggles streaking shafts of light slammed into their targets; white fireballs exploded at the end of their laser beam straightness. The streaks of seeming laser light happened in rapid succession, one after another after another. The tracer like M1A1 sabot rounds piercing the atmosphere, accentuated by my infrared night vision, created a horrific scene of fire in the valley. As artillery boomed constantly somewhere very near, the steadily increasing noise of the battle seemed to reach a crescendo. The incredible succession of rapid tank fire roared up at us like waves; the chaos and mayhem threatening to overwhelm my senses.

I looked over at Sergeant T as he held the lit cigarette under his poncho. Neither of us spoke. I followed the vehicle at my front, into the valley.

Chapter 16
Valley of Death

Yea, though I walk through the valley of the shadow of death, I will fear no evil: for thou art with me; thy rod and thy staff they comfort me.

Thou preparest a table before me in the presence of mine enemies: thou anointest my head with oil; my cup runneth over.

Surely goodness and mercy shall follow me all the days of my life: and I will dwell in the house of the Lord forever.

23rd Psalm:

The 23rd Psalm would have been a good prayer for me to say as Sergeant T and I descended into that valley. Though it was terrifying as hell driving down into the middle of a fiery mess, I knew that whatever happened from this point on was in the hands of something larger than myself. I also remember the crazy exhilaration at the edge of my emotions. "This was it, man!" We were driving into the middle of battle. I knew as I descended that hill that this moment would be etched into my memory forever. This moment was every warrior's dream.

Descending the hill the laser light and booming fireball show continued unabated. As we closed in I estimated the main battle was some two, maybe three kilometers to our front. As we reached the bottom of the hill, and with the suddenness of switching off a light, the cannon fire ceased. Minutes later, traveling through the valley floor, smoldering and burning Republican Guard tanks, trucks, and pc's were all that remained. Most were burning a short distance to our south, we weaved between others that were in our path. The stinking sulfur smell of spent tank rounds, the sooty stink of burning fuel, electronic components, and burning steel filled the valley floor. Sergeant T and I were without words as we drove through it. I could only catch continual quick glances at the carnage as I reminded myself to stay in the tracks of the vehicle to my front.

HQ-26

The story about the scout crew in the Bradley fighting vehicle, HQ-26, was circulating in the battalion. They'd been hit about 24 hours ago and were the Red Lions only loss up to this point. Most of this story is compiled from a People Magazine article in which my scout buddy Frank Bradish (Scout Dude) tells his story.

There were six Bradley's in the Red Lion scout platoon. Each of them traveled about a mile and a half apart as they probed for the enemy the night of the 26th. The M3 version of the Bradley, designed for the scout, has a crew of five. A driver, a gunner and commander who ride in the circling turret at the middle of the vehicle, and two dismounts who ride in the crew compartment at the rear. HQ-26 came upon a T-72 Republican Guard tank at close range and made the decision to fire its 25mm gun. The T-72 fired back with its main gun, hitting 26 and setting off a deadly chain of events. PFC Frank Bradish (Scout Dude) was a dismount riding in the rear of the Bradley with PFC Adrian Stokes, the other dismount crew member. The T-72 round set off the halon fire extinguisher system in the Bradley, prompting Scout Dude to open the rear door of the Bradley. Upon opening the door he was shot through both thighs, losing a testicle and part of his fingers. He was hit by either .50 caliber or Soviet 12.7mm rounds. The bullets ripped through stokes, severing both his legs. Rounds of .50 caliber go through steel like butter. They tore into the turret area of the Bradley, setting off an ammunition box which sprayed exploding ammunition through the turret, killing the commander, Staff Sergeant Christopher Stephans, instantly. The gunner somehow was thrown free from the turret and suffered a sucking chest wound. In the meantime, still able to move, Scout Dude pulled Stokes out of the vehicle to some safety at its side. He then went to look for the rest of the crew, crawling on top of the Bradley to see the commander cut to pieces, but not finding the gunner or the driver. He went back inside for flares, a radio, and an M-60 machine gun. After securing these and returning to the side of the Bradley he heard a moaning in the moonless pitch blackness and found the gunner about 50 feet away. He dragged the chest wounded gunner back to his area and set up a small perimeter.

He tried to call out a distress message on the small back-packed PRC-77 radio he had pulled from the Bradley, but there was so much radio traffic at the time the low wattage signal of the PRC-77 could not override the other traffic. Realizing why he couldn't get through on the radio, he found a white cluster distress flare, but his fingers were too mangled to pull the top off the flare. He succeeded by using his teeth. As soon as the flare went up the scout commander gave the order to clear the radio net and that's when Scout Dude got his distress message through.

All this time they were taking small arms fire from the front and opposite sides of the Bradley. Finally the driver came around the vehicle in a daze. He had, incredibly, not been wounded. Scout Dude and the driver returned fire with the M-60 machine gun and an M-203 grenade launcher (an M-16 with a 40mm grenade launcher attached). This went on for approximately 20 minutes, at which time the rest of the scout platoon and Red Lion medics arrived to secure the area and take care of the dead and wounded.

Staff Sergeant Stephans died at the scene. PFC Stokes died from loss of blood at the battalion medical aid station. The gunner made it and so did the driver. Scout Dude made it out too. For his actions in saving his fellow crew members, and his bravery, he received the Silver Star.

I hadn't seen much of Sergeant Milano since coming to the desert. Our commo comrade had been assigned to battalion headquarters and was separated from us a lot. We saw him every couple of days for a few minutes when we went to battalion HQ to transport equipment. Being with battalion HQ he was much closer to the action than we were and had the dubious honor of being Colonel Cramer's personal radio man. Everywhere the colonel went Sergeant Milano was not far behind, battle or not.

During the most intense action of the battle Sergeant Milano was in an unprotected humvee only a few hundred feet behind the colonel .... who was in a tank. When he told me his story about the battle going on all around him, and being only in a hummer, I told him he was nuts for not being in some kind of armored vehicle.

On the night of the 27th Sergeant Milano and a young private were in their position just 100 feet behind Colonel Cramer's tank. The tank was firing rounds at Iraqi targets, Apache attack choppers were flying directly overhead, stopping, pointing their noses downward and firing streams of white streaking rockets into enemy armor. Sergeant Milano said it was a show like nothing he'd ever seen. The funny part of this story is that the young private assigned to accompany him in the humvee slept through the whole thing! Rockets were flying overhead, booming tank rounds roared from their cannons only hundreds of feet away, and this kid's dead to the world.

Sergeant Milano lit another cigarette as he finished telling me his story, "Christ, it'd only taken one machine gun round sneaking through to blow us to bits. Either the kid had nerves of steel, or no nerves at all."

For his bravery in following a tank, in a humvee, through battle, Sergeant Milano was awarded the Bronze Star.

Charlie-32

Sergeant Summerall and the three young men who made up the rest of the crew in the M1A1 Abrams main battle tank designated Charlie-32, were part of 3rd platoon, Charlie Company of the Red Lions tank battalion. Sergeant Summerall was the platoon sergeant of this four tank platoon. He sat in the elevated commanders seat which took up the right rear corner in the circling turret sitting atop the main body of this 63 ton, 1500 horsepower monster. From his position in the turret he had night vision optical sights with a range of 3000 meters directly at his front, and control of a .50 caliber machine gun located above him atop the turret. His gunner sat ahead and below him in the lowest part of the cramped quarters. Through the on-board intercom system, he relayed orders to the gunner and the rest of the crew as 32 closed in on enemy armor to their front. The gunner had control of the 120 mm main cannon and a 7.62 coaxial sub-machine gun located next to the cannon. They were to spew forth death and destruction the night of the 27th.

As the 3rd platoon, along with the rest of the Red Lions, rolled into that valley this night the thermal sensors on their night vision equipment began picking up the heat signatures of many, many vehicles in the south and southeast end of this long, flat valley. Earlier reconnaissance had confirmed this was Iraqi Republican Guard armor, in particular, part of the Tawakalna Division, and now the night vision gave confirmation as the distinct outline of the Soviet T-72 battle tank came into clear view.

As 32 rolled into range some one and one-half miles from these targets, the order came through from Colonel Kramer at battalion HQ to engage enemy armor. In Sergeant Summerall's sights, directly ahead, an Iraqi armored personnel carrier sat at idle, its warm engine heat signature showing through the night vision. Sergeant Summerall, Master Gunner, felt the pulse hammering through his veins. This was it. All the training had come down to this moment.

"Bring us to a stop," he ordered the driver, who sat in the forward part of the main body of the vehicle. "You got that pc?," he asked his gunner, his voice quite calm at the onset. "Got him, Sarge," the gunner called back as his laser range finding equipment locked in the direction, elevation and distance to the target in an instant. "HEAT!," Sergeant Summerall yelled next through his intercom, instructing the loader standing to his left on the other side of the cannon, which angled through the center of the turret, to load the phosphorous metal burning round into the rear of the cannon. "UP!," the young loader yelled into his microphone not four seconds later. "ON THE WAY!," the gunner yelled, pulling the hand held trigger on his left. The tank lurched back from the loosing of the round. Inside, only a metallic "Clink, Clink" sound was heard as the cannon recoiled some two feet to the far rear of the turret. A fiery white fireball was seen instantly in Sergeant Summerall's sight. "T-72 at 11 o'clock coming from behind that bunker!," he yelled at his gunner. "Got him, Sarge!," the gunner, now blood pounding through his brain, yelled back. "Driver, move us out to flank him, 2 o'clock!" As the M1A1 lurched forward and gained speed Sergeant Summerall swung the turret toward the enemy. The gunner lased on the target and coordinates were fed instantly into the brain of the tartgeting mechanism. The same fire orders were given. This time it was the armor piercing Sabot round he unleashed at his enemy. At

25 miles per hour the accuracy of the round was undiminished. Another white fireball again greeted him at the destruction of the T-72.

When this part of the battle was concluded, not ten minutes later, two more T-72's and another pc lay smoldering from rounds loosed by Sergeant Summerall and his crew. The reports I saw credited Summerall with six enemy tank kills, five pc kills, and numerous artillery and truck kills during the entire length of the war. No one in the battalion had higher numbers. In the 3rd Armored Division, few saw heavier action than the Red Lions. In Tom Clancy's book *Armored Cav,* Clancy comments on the Gulf War and the M1A1 Abrams tank:

> "For the record, M1A1's killed more enemy tanks than any other weapons system of the war. 'When I went into Kuwait I had thirty nine tanks,' one captured Iraqi battalion commander said. 'After six weeks of air bombardment, I had thrity two left. After twenty minutes in action against the M1's, I had none.'"

As we drove on into the night the speed of the convoy increased, sometimes 40 miles per hour and more. In the pitch blackness I drove, seeing through my night vision the tracks of the truck at my front and his rear black out drive lights. Flashes of light, streaking shafts from rocket attacks, and an occasional crash of thunder got through over the noise of the hummer. We were in the main assembly areas for the Republican Guard. Huge, built up mounds of sand were everywhere. Holes had been dug into the ground for armored vehicles to help shield them from air attack. In the holes I could see the outline of blown up tanks and artillery pieces. The mounds were absolutely everywhere, and we drove for miles and miles through the littered landscape of armored tanks, pc's, trucks, and artillery; all blown to bits. Some were cold, having been hit by previous air attack, some were burning and smoldering from the rolling ground assault.

At about 0300 hours, 28 February, after driving all night, Sergeant T and I came upon a berm. It was the same type of piled up dirt I had seen at the Iraqi-Saudi border. I didn't know it at the time, but this was the border into Kuwait. The division had made the sweep completely through Iraq at this point and we were now headed into Kuwait at approximately the northern tip of the country.

There were no bulldozers to clear a path through this berm, so we had to drive over it. The smaller vehicles had no problem, but as Sergeant T and I approached in the hummer a long ammunition carrying hemmit became stuck in the sand. We waited for him to get out but he was having little luck. After five minutes of waiting a hummer to our front took another path around him and other vehicles followed. As we approached I cleared the berm with little problem. As I came over the top and back down the other side there was no vehicle to follow. I looked for the tracks of vehicles that had preceded us but there were tire tracks in every direction. I pulled ahead 100 meters or so from the berm and stopped, looking through my night vision for some sign of the vehicles that must have been to our front. Way off at about 11 o'clock, I believed I could see the small taillights from someone's black out drive. Sergeant T didn't have his night vision on at the time. He asked me what I could see.

"Put your night vision on, Sarge. I think I see black out drive lights up about a mile or so."

He got his goggles on. "I don't see a goddamn thing."

He was right because as soon as I turned back to look again the lights were gone. "I'm pretty damn sure I saw those lights, Sergeant T. Let's head that direction."

"Wait a minute." He scanned the whole area and by this time

other vehicles had come up to our rear and stopped. "Listen, I don't see a fuckin' thing. Don't you get any crazy ideas about driving us off into someplace and we don't know what the hell is out there."

"Sarge, I'm damn sure I saw those lights out there, they must have either pulled ahead or shut down." I thought about being stranded and then who knows what could happen. Being stranded and left behind this fast moving battle was one of my biggest fears. I dropped the vehicle into drive and started pulling ahead.

"What the fuck are you doing? Stay right here! We got a god-damn battle going on all around us and you want to drive off not knowing where the fuck we're going? We don't know what the hell's out there. You park this son-of-a-bitch right here and don't move! Somebody will figure out we're gone."

My instincts told me the rest of the convoy was up there, but Sergeant T knew what he saw too. Nothing. "Okay," I said. Sergeant T was uptight, and so was I. It was an incredible moment of indecision. He was in charge and my training told me I had better heed the order he'd just given me. The loaded .45 he carried popped into my mind all of a sudden. I parked the vehicle.

We waited at idle while Sergeant T lit a Winston under his rain poncho. Flashes of light were going off to our south and I could hear some small arms fire from that direction. The night was pitch black and there was nobody around. I thought about Iraqi tanks coming from the direction of the flashing lights and blowing us to shit while we waited for the rest of the convoy .... Did I imagine seeing those tail lights? What the hell happened to those guys? Minutes passed ....

"Where the hell did everybody go?" It was the driver of the cargo hemmit which had been stuck in the sand.

I unzipped the soft plastic window of the hummer. "I don't

know, man. I thought I saw black out drive lights up ahead about a mile, but now there ain't shit."

"Okay, let's go."

The cargo driver jumped back into his hemmit and pulled around us. I hesitantly reached over to drop the hummer into drive.

"Don't even think about it! Jesus Christ!" I took my hand away from the shift, pulled my rain poncho over my head and lit a cigarette. The hemmit pulled ahead about 100 meters and stopped, seeing us not follow .... Grueling minutes passed as we waited in silence. We were naked, in the middle of a battle. I had an M-16, Sergeant T a .45. The enemy had T-72's with 120mm guns. The hummer sat idling while the flashing white light to our south kept up steadily. The small arms fire waded in over the noise of the hummer and low booms from the flashing lights were heard way off. We waited.

"Jesus, where the hell are those bastards? How the hell'd they get ahead of us that fuckin' fast?" At least he was talking.

"I don't know, Sergeant T. I came over the berm and nothing, not a goddamn thing. I can't believe it." I'd been searching the whole time through my night vision. Nothing. Time slowly crept by. Ten minutes so far had seemed like ten hours. Another slow ten minutes. We didn't move. Then, as I looked through my night vision I saw the small lights of an approaching vehicle. It was heading toward us. This had better be friendly was all I could think. We'd driven through so much blown up shit all night and seen firepower unleashed on such a scale that in my mind our little hummer seemed like a speck of dust on the desert landscape. An approaching T-72 would exert little effort in eliminating our asses. It was a vehicle coming at us for sure. As it approached I made out the familiar lines of a hummer through my night vision. Sure enough, it was First Sergeant Dillon. Here was a man whom I loathed most of the time, but this night I loved the son-of-a-bitch. "What the hell happened?" he asked as I zipped down the drivers side plastic window.

"We came over the berm and not a goddamn thing was in front of us," both Sergeant T and I blurted. I felt like we were a couple of lost kids and there was mom to rescue us; it wasn't a bad feeling.

"Alright, follow me." His voice had a nasal monotone that drove me crazy most of the time; this night it sounded like a choir.

We followed Top to the place where I had seen the lights. It was about a one mile drive. I didn't say anything to Sergeant T and the incident was never brought up again between us while we were in the Gulf. We'd talk about it over a beer much later. I looked at my watch and it was 0400 hours. The whole convoy was stopped around us at idle. Word was given to shut down so I killed the hummer and slumped down in my seat. The rat-tat-tat of automatic weapon fire in the distance lulled me to a quick sleep.

I awoke about 0730 hours the morning of the 28th. I threw on my web gear and Kevlar helmet and stepped out of the hummer for a stretch. A gray sky again; the same muck we'd been in the past four days. Sergeant Thompson had been out of the hummer ahead of me and came back with a cup of coffee. He told me the cooks had coffee and hot soup up front. We talked like our disagreement from last night had never occurred. I challenged Sergeant T a lot and this incident was no exception. He was the type of leader who didn't need, even des-pised people he considered "yes men." I think he thrived on people challenging his decisions; mostly because he was usually right. My ever-questioning attitude seemed to be why we'd been a team for two and a half years at this point. "Get a cup of coffee, Jones."

"On my way."

I came back to the hummer and leaned on the hood, drinking

army coffee, which tasted like it'd been in the plastic urns they used to dispense the stuff much too long. I surveyed the landscape. The mounds of earth from the dug-in Iraqi positions were all around us. Blown up tanks, pc's, and other vehicles were everywhere, I mean everywhere. A junkyard as far as I could see, and in every direction. Sporadic automatic weapon fire still went on in the distance. For the last day or so I had become convinced we were going to Baghdad. I just felt with all this machinery moving at once we would keep going and eliminate the problem called Saddam Hussein. The success of our move through Iraq was stunning and apparent all around me.

Sergeant T said we were in Kuwait. "No kidding? When did we get here?"

"That berm was the border."

"It seems to me we're going to Baghdad ...." Before he could answer me Captain Hanks came out of his pc and yelled at the top of his lungs "Cease Fire! A cease fire has been ordered effective 0800 hours, 28 February, 1991 gentlemen!! Y'all get a cup of coffee." I looked at my watch. It said 0800 exactly.

Part III

Chapter 17
Ceasefire!

A thick, dark, cloudy haze covered the mono-colored desert as I looked out over the destruction wrought around our position. Tanks and pc's smoldering in the distance added to the soupy grayness above us. Relief flooded through me. We'd made it! Some gave a yell at the CO's announcement, but most just stood stunned. I couldn't believe it had happened that fast. "Let's get the hell out of this desert!" I thought, but I knew it would take months before all that equipment and manpower made it out. We were one of the last units in, we would be one of the last out.

The MOPP status was dropped to level one immediately, and a few hours later dropped to level zero. Walking around without the heavy charcoal suit made the load much lighter; we'd been in them for four days. The pill taking stopped; I thanked God.

I walked over to inspect a blown Iraqi tank about 50 meters from our position. Even though we had driven all night through a destroyed army, this was my first close-up view of a destroyed vehicle. In the coming months I would see hundreds this close, but the first one is a shock. It was a T-60 Soviet model tank; massively, completely destroyed. It had been dug into the sand, about turret level, and since it was not smoldering, and rust covered some of the metal bits and pieces around it, it had probably been hit during air strikes that had occurred in this area before we'd arrived. The surrounding desert was pock marked with bomb craters, with the particular bomb that had taken out this tank being pinpoint accurate. In my mind I tried to imagine the explosion it took to do what had been done to this tank. The turret was blown completely off the main body of the tank and lay four or five meters to the side, completely intact. The engine, also intact, lay ten meters to the rear of the vehicle on the desert floor. There was nothing that would indicate anyone had been inside when it was hit. There were obviously no survivors if there had been. Blown apart ammo boxes with spent and unspent ammunition were strewn to the sides and rear of the hole where the tank sat. It was a sobering sight. After word of the ceasefire, the euphoria was short lived; devastation surrounded me.

At about 1200 hours the word came to move. It was not a long road march; about fifteen kilometers to a stationary position just inside Kuwait. Headquarters company of the Red Lions, along with other support elements in our brigade, broke off from the rest of the combat units and set up positions in the rear. We were told we'd be in this position for some time. Sergeant T and I found a place for our vehicle and pulled a small hex tent from the back of the hummer .... It was something to call home anyway.

There had been explosions going on all morning, and these would continue for weeks as we blew up thousands of abandoned vehicles littering the area. The destruction of Hussein's military hardware would keep it out of Iraqi hands after we left. We'd let them have the left-over scrap iron. News filtered in about how the decision was made to stop the war. Of the eight divisions of Republican Guard troops that VII Corps had engaged in the end around run through Iraq and northern Kuwait, two were left intact, and they were infantry divisions. What was left of the rest were battalion sized elements or nothing at all. Official figures, listed on February 28th in the Washington Post, claimed that since the beginning of hostilities in January 3,700 Iraqi tanks were destroyed out of a total of 4,230; 2,140 artillery pieces destroyed out of a total of 3,110; and 35,000 EPW's were taken on the northern battlefield.

In seeing, hearing, and feeling this battle, I believe the decision to stop our engagement of the Republican Guard, and the rest of the Iraqi army, was made because of the slaughter of a hapless enemy. Most gave up upon seeing us, but many didn't, and those who didn't were cut down. From my perspective, our battle as part of VII Corps and the 3rd Armored Division lasted 36 hours. The ground war as a whole lasted 100 hours, but we did not engage until the night of the 26th. In that 36 hours we destroyed a massive army. We cut down his supposedly finest and most feared with terrifying and ferocious ease.

I also believe a political decision was made to leave part of his army intact in order not to leave a complete vacuum of power in the region. I was a soldier during this and not a politician. Soldier's carry our politician's orders. But I remember my feelings at the time. We were slaughtering an army and we all knew it. As stated earlier, I thanked God when it stopped.

"You got the cots inside and got us dug in?" I'd been working a good part of that afternoon getting set up and digging foxhole positions.

"Yeah. Didn't get the hole dug very deep. I'll hit it some more later on tonight." Sergeant T had been at battalion HQ most of the afternoon for briefings and such. We were sitting in the hummer just about evening chow time. He poured a cup of coffee from his thermos.

"They put the numbers out up there."

"They did?"

"The Red Lions took out 200 enemy tanks, 150 pc's, a whole hell of a lot of artillery, trucks, and other shit."

"No kidding?" I listened between bites of cold spaghetti from my MRE pack.

"Yeah." He took a drink from his coffee cup. "The battalion took 3,000 EPW's and had 2,000 enemy kills .... "

I stuck my plastic spoon into the cold spaghetti and felt the numbness settle in. My face felt hot. Sergeant T stated those last figures robotically, staring straight ahead. Neither of us spoke for a long few minutes. I could see the numbness had settled on Sergeant T also. Our little battalion of 58 tanks had killed 2000 men in less than 36 hours. We both stared straight ahead a while longer while I finished the MRE.

"Coffee?"

"Thanks."

The strained silence between Sergeant T and I at his announcement of those numbers says something about the mixed feelings I had. On the one hand we had all just witnessed the most awesome display of brute, raw power any of us had ever seen. Even though we were not on the receiving end, the display was overwhelming to the point of terror. I felt the power of that display and pride and cockiness at how awesome our inventions are. We were some bad-ass boys. On the other hand I began to see this whole exercise as making an excuse for future generations to make a decision for war when maybe other solutions might exist. Would people think that war was now an easy task?

About the numbers I mentioned. My battalion logistics people kept track of every enemy soldier captured or killed by our combat personnel. The radios constantly report this information to battalion. Oftentimes the decision was made by the battalion commander whether to engage enemy personnel or not. Many radio conversations were of the sort saying, "Yeah, Red Lion six (battalion commander), we've got ten enemy personnel running from two abandoned pc's, carrying personal weapons." In this case the decision was made by the commander whether or not to engage. If these soldiers did not show clear signs of surrender, or were perceived as a threat of any kind, they were cut down. If enemy soldiers were engaged, the number of killed, captured, or wounded was always reported to battalion. The logisticians job is to keep track of those numbers. The Red Lions were one of 15 combat battalions in the 3rd Armored Division. The Red Lions spearheaded First Brigade and First Brigade spearheaded the division. We saw more action than most, but overall we were only a small part. There were, at least, six full combat divisions in VII Corps.

That evening Sergeant Hawkins (Hayseed) from Charlie company commo pulled up in his commander's hummer. He had driven in from the main part of the battalion, which was set up about ten kilometers north toward the Iraqi border.

"You two get a chance to check out any of the bunkers in this area?"

"Nope." Sergeant T replied. "We had to get our asses set up first."

Sergeant Hawkins had shut off the hummer and was lazily leaning out its open door window. "You got to check out what's up there. Our first sergeant has a fully working AK-47. There's berets, uniforms, gas masks, radios. Everything was left in those bunkers. They left in a hell of a hurry."

"You found radios? Jesus, I'd like to get hold of an Iraqi radio for a souvenir." Sergeant T was a little more interested.

"Yeah, we found a whole bunker full of commo equipment. The LT (Lieutenant Moore from battalion commo) has a working FM radio."

"No shit?"

"Yeah, no shit. You seen any of those blown-out tanks yet?"

"Not yet."

"We found one guy burned to a crisp. Was the driver of a T-72. It looks like he was fried so fast he didn't know what hit him. His hands were melted to the steering wheel."

Both Sergeant T and I grunted.

"Some pretty gruesome sights out there."

"I don't know if I want to see it or not," I jumped in.

Sergeant Hawkins looked over at me. I was leaning in the passenger window listening to the conversation. "Maybe it's something everybody should see."

"Maybe."

The next day Lieutenant Moore came over and asked if we wanted to go with him to inspect the bunkers in the area. He talked excitedly about the incredible number of bunkers and the amount of equipment, especially communications, he'd seen in them. Sergeant T and I jumped at the chance.

As we drove through the brigade area and toward the front where the Republican Guard divisions had been dug in, I began to see earthen mounds everywhere. For miles on end, horizon to horizon, there were piles of dirt where holes had been dug to give the tanks and artillery a lower profile. The bunkers where the troops lived were also dug deep into the sand. I could see most of them had makeshift tin roofs; personal belongings strewn all around them.

There were spent munitions everywhere as we snaked among the mounds and bunkers. The LT told us there were unexploded cluster bombs here; leftovers from the massive number of multiple launch rockets fired into the Republican Guard divisions. One rocket contained hundreds of these bomblets. They were about the size of a baseball; designed to take out personnel. Most exploded on contact with the earth, but some didn't. Any contact could set one off. If a person happened to move or kick one he or she would probably be killed. If we hit one with the hummer we would probably survive, unless shrapnel pierced the floor of the hummer. Jackson, the bookish wiredog from commo, was driving. Jackson was smart so I had faith in him. We drove around anything that even looked suspicious, making a lot of quick sharp turns in the middle of nowhere.

We reached a set of bunkers where the LT said to stop. We jumped out of the hummer and walked carefully up to them. I walked around the spent munitions littering the ground and peered down into one of the cavernous bunkers. Green Iraqi army uniforms, helmets, combat boots, gasmasks, and ammunition all littered the entrance to the bunker. Steps had been cut out of the sand, descending about six feet into the earth. A corrugated tin roof covered the bunker, which I estimated to be about ten feet by ten feet in width and length.

I saw everyone else walking into other bunkers around me, so I descended. It was dark inside and a dank musty odor from wood timbers used in the bunker's construction, along with clothing all made wet by the recent rains, permeated the structure. As my eyes adjusted to the light I looked around at a ransacked living area. I made out wooden bunks, some with mattress padding, some without, blankets, papers, and cardboard boxes containing books. I picked up what seemed to be a journal. It was handwritten in Arabic and seemed personal. I turned over some of the military hardware in the bunker, gas masks and helmets. It seemed obvious everyone had left this place on a very short notice. The gas masks left behind seemed to point this out. We went nowhere without our gas masks.

I grabbed an Iraqi helmet, gas mask, and the journal as I walked out of the bunker into the bright sunlight that day. I looked over at Sergeant T who had a yellow duffel bag with a Republican Guard insignia (a triangle with Arabic numbers inscribed in it) on the side. He had the duffel bag almost full of Iraqi personal belongings. The stuff was absolutely everywhere. It looked like the area had been looted, either by GI's who had been here before us or the Guard troops as they left. "Let's move to another area!," the LT yelled, "I want to find that communications bunker."

We jumped into the hummer and again headed out across the littered landscape. Hundreds, maybe thousands of destroyed vehicles of all types were scattered over the desert in this area. Some in the dug out holes, others not. There was little if anything intact. An abandoned pc occasionally could be seen untouched as we drove through mile after mile of complete destruction.

We came upon another set of bunkers where other GI's were picking through Iraqi belongings. As we approached we made out Sergeant Major Dickinson from battalion S-3 (logistics). He had a Russian AK-47 assault rifle with a shiny bayonet attached. There were AK's everywhere, but mostly they were in poor shape, with some in pieces.

We toured these bunkers finding much of the same. I grabbed a Republican Guard duffel bag and started throwing in other little trinkets: a talc powder container with a pretty woman's face painted on its side; more books, all in Arabic; spent and unspent ammunition (later we had to get rid of all the ammunition and weapons we had confiscated). Also in this area were cans of Kraft cheese; little tins about the size of tuna fish cans with the Kraft label in English and Arabic! It was the only food I could see in these areas. I saw little evidence to contradict the stories of starving soldiers. There were places where pots had been set up to collect the rain water as it came off the corrugated tin roofs of the bunkers. I had heard the story that a few weeks before the beginning of the ground war new recruits were brought into this area with only the food and water they had brought from home; this would be all they would have. Stories that some soldiers had only seeds to eat from the sagebrush-like weeds that dotted the area were common.

Maybe the Kraft cheese was someone's supply from home.

I loaded the Republican Guard duffel bag full of Iraqi equipment. We found the communications bunker and both Sergeant T and I took out small backpacked radios, remarkably like our own PRC-77 backpack type radios. They had a Made-in-Britain sticker with all the numbers and letters printed in Arabic. I had a feeling like the warriors of old must have had as they pillaged the belongings of conquered nations or peoples. We rummaged through everything we saw, taking anything that seemed to have value. We were conquerors, victors. To the victor goes the spoils.

We made it back to the company assembly area and threw all of our booty into the tent. Many in the platoon hadn't had the chance to get out to see the bunkers, so guys wanted to see what I had. I gave a bunch of it away. I began to feel, the longer I kept the booty, that it was tainted. It wasn't really my property. These were the belongings of dead men, men we'd killed. It was a feeling in my gut when I looked at it. Unsettling. Horror. I kept the journal and a few other trinkets, giving everything else away. The radio, and a beret I picked up later, were shipped by Sergeant T to his home in Germany. I always intended to get these from him but have yet to do it.

A few days after we'd toured the bunkers an order came down from the CO that we could no longer go into those areas. Some of the bunkers had been booby trapped; GI's had been killed checking them out. The CO also told us it was extremely hazardous to drive around out there. Well, we already knew that.

A captain from our higher support battalion in the brigade was killed a week or so after the cease fire; drove his humvee over a land mine. I looked back to that day and thought about the risk we took driving around out there. But hey, after just surviving a war, what were a few cluster bombs?

Chapter 18
Back to Iraq

It was a bright, sunny day in northern Kuwait. If my eyes stayed focused on the clear blue sky and not the barren landscape all around me, it was almost cheery. I was staring at the battalion commander's M-1A1 tank, parked alongside the battalion XO's tank; both 120mm main gun barrels pointed above the heads myself and the rest of the Red Lions. The company commanders and the battalion commander were seated in front of the tanks along with the chaplain. A Blackhawk helicopter flew over and someone whispered it was the general. The Blackhawk landed about a hundred feet to the right of our gathering and Major General Funk, 3rd Armored Division commander, stepped out. Up to this point I'd never been that close to a general. From my position generals were a long way up the chain of command. He was a regular looking guy. As he walked past to take his chair with the rest of the commanders, I noticed the creases on his neck; like leather.

The chaplain arose and said a prayer. "I don't know why some leave us and some stay," he said. "That's a question we can't answer. Remember these men. They were your friends."

Two soldiers from the scout platoon got up next and talked about Staff Sergeant Stephans and Private First Class Stokes. Sergeant Stephans went way back in the battalion. Sergeant Burgess and Sergeant T had worked with Sergeant Stephans everyday for five or six years. I looked to my right where top gunner Sergeant Summerall sat. I could read no expression on his face and wondered how battle had changed my academy instructor. Sergeant T was sitting next to me stonefaced, hiding any emotion. Grief over the loss of a friend would come later, when there was time to think about loss.

Captain Hanks got up to speak after the scouts took their seats. Captain Hanks' emotions were always close to the surface. That's how the CO was. I know he loved every last stinking one of us. I remembered with a chill the prophetic speech he'd given before we left for the desert, about knowing not all of us were coming back from this place. As he stood, the wind snapped the colors which were planted next to the tanks. He started his remarks, very calmly, completing one sentence. As the second sentence came his voice broke up. Each word seemed to push him toward uncontrollable tears. By the end of the sentence he was crying like a baby. I don't know if I have ever seen a man break up that hard. He continued on, though, stopping momentarily to gain control, but each new word brought wrenching sobs. He blurted that he was sorry and put his shaking hands to his face. He turned around and walked into the desert. As we watched in silence, the Charlie company CO jumped up and walked toward Captain Hanks, putting an arm around him as they walked.

After a few moments General Funk got up to speak. I saw his face close up for the first time. The leather quality on the back of his neck was etched as well on his forehead and around his eyes and mouth. He took off his Kevlar helmet and I noticed he was balding a bit, with tufts of gray hair on the side. If ever I pictured what a general should look like, here he was. His tough exterior melted and a look of decency crossed his face, even humility. I saw the moisture in his eyes as he started to speak. "You know, I was in Vietnam." He walked back and forth in front of us, then took his left hand and started pointing to the back of his head, pressing a finger into the leather on his neck. "I still got some of those guys running around back here." He paused, the tears ran down the valleys on his cheeks. 500 Red Lions sat completely still, only the wind could be heard snapping at the colors. "It's alright to cry you know. These men, Staff Sergeant Stephans and Private First Class Stokes, you will never forget ...." He paused and touched his face, completely regaining his composure.

"You know, I just saw something I could have never seen in Vietnam. Did you see that white captain put his arm around that black captain. That is something I want each and every one of you here to remember. As different as each of us are, we can put that aside and do our jobs. That is why we are the greatest fighting force on earth. It has been an honor and a privilege to serve as commander of this great 3rd Armored Division, and of you 4th of the 32nd. The Red Lions."

A few minutes after General Funk finished his speech, Captain Hanks came back and took his place up front. A few small speeches came after that, with the chaplain ending the ceremony. The General's Blackhawk flew back overhead leaving us to go about the rest of our day.

The General's speech reminded me that the color of a person's skin meant very little in the army. Not that racism doesn't exist in the army, I just saw very little of it. The CO was the most respected man in our company, and it didn't matter that he was a black man, he was our leader. It was his rank and the content of his character that defined the man. In my army experience there was never any hint that one soldier had an advantage over another because of race. I perceived a level playing field in which a black kid from East Saint Louis, as long as he or she had the basic skills and the drive to educate him or herself, had just as much chance for advancement as a white midwestern farmboy like myself. That level playing field has eliminated some of the animosity that being out in the "real world" generates. Maybe racism is a by-product of the way we live. The system in which we are dependent upon for our living may have a need for division among peoples. A group divided will be much less likely to, say, argue for higher wages. It would seem obvious that an army which is divided will not work nearly as well as it could. Can any organization, political, economic, or otherwise, possibly work as well as it could, if it continues to remain divided?

New Mission

During the first week in March we let surrendered Iraqi troops pass through our lines, back into Iraq. An Iraqi pc pulled into our area one day displaying a huge orange flag; the flag signaling it could pass through our lines. Some in my unit reported seeing the Hind helicopter (A Russian attack chopper which Iraq had) pass overhead. These were the gunships which would be used in the suppression of the rebellious Shiite Moslems in southern Iraq. Immediately after the ceasefire the Shiites began their rebellion against Saddam thinking they would get U.S. support. That support never came. The generals even went so far as to let Iraq keep their helicopter gunships after the war in what General Schwarzkopf described as an oversight. Their oversight had devastating consequences for the rebelling Shiites. How the decision was made on what equipment would be destroyed and what would be let back to Iraq I do not know. We were destroying abandoned tanks and pc's all over the area, but on this day we let an armored personnel carrier pass through our lines. Without question we laid waste to a huge part of his army, but Hussein's ability to squash those rebellions made it increasingly obvious we had not destroyed it all.

The uprising by the Shiites during that first part of March occurred in an area not far from our location in northern Kuwait. The majority of the fighting was in and around the southern city of Basra, Iraq's second largest city. 3rd Armored Division, along with the whole of VII Corps, held a secured area all the way from northern Kuwait well into southern Iraq, approximately to the Euphrates river valley. We could neither see nor hear the fighting about 50 or so miles to our north, but GI's in that area had to witness this fighting without interfering. I had a conversation with a 2nd Armored Cavalry Regiment soldier after the war. His unit was in the area around Basra and he talked of watching an artillery attack on a town outside the city and having to go in afterward to give aid. Women and children had been killed indiscriminately by the falling shells; he had to pull their bodies from the rubble. He did not paint a pretty picture. I could see the violence which occurred after the war had affected him more than the war itself. Also during this time remnants of Hussein's Republican Guard were going house to house in the Shiite region executing all males over the age of 15.

It became increasingly obvious during the first two weeks after the ceasefire that in no way shape or form was our job done in this place, nor were we removed from the possibility of being involved in more fighting. Rumors were rampant that we were about to head north into the Basra region and my heart sank when on 11 March we were given orders that the Red Lions, and the Red Lions alone, would be leaving this part of Kuwait and heading north to a region just outside Basra. We would hook up with 2nd Brigade, 3rd Armor, when we arrived. The Red Lions previous reputation as a crack bunch of tankers, along with our success during the war, got us this assignment. We had to move the battalion 50 to 75 miles straight north in about a day's time. There we would dig in while helping provide security for other parts of our division in the area. While a war raged around us we would be providing support to help destroy one of the largest munitions dumps I had ever seen, or heard of. 200,000 tons of Iraqi munitions were in the area we were heading toward. I packed my bags wondering if I'd just been lucky to make it this far. I remembered the relief I'd felt at the calling of the ceasefire. No relief now. Only the familiar knot in the stomach feeling of danger. I was real happy General Funk thought we were such a good unit. Thanks General.

It was 14 March when we pulled out of northern Kuwait and headed for the border of Iraq. Sergeant T and I had lost our hummer back to the air force boys just the day before. The parts to fix it never did come and the air force guys finally got wise, seeing us drive the thing around every day. It was inevitable we'd eventually lose the thing. I caught a ride as shotgun on a deuce-and-a-half.

As we progressed toward the border we traveled through the devastated battlefields where we had fought the Republican Guard. It was at least a 50 mile march to our position just west of Basra, and there was not one of those miles in which I did not see destroyed Iraqi tanks, pc's, artillery pieces, or trucks. A literal junkyard for as far as the eye could see. We approached a built-up sand berm with a paved road straddling it. I guessed that this was the border. As we crossed I could smell the stench of rotting flesh. Engineer's bulldozers were in the distance. It seemed here the devastation was greatest. A toppled radio tower could be seen off to the east, and in numerous places there were circular formations of trucks and other support vehicles blown to bits or burned to a crisp where they sat. We snaked through unexploded munitions which were scattered everywhere. On one of our stops Sergeant T went to investigate a burned-out pc. A torched skull greeted him, rolling to the ground at his feet as he opened the back door of the vehicle.

As we crossed the border I noticed the skies were an eerie purplish black. Though there were 900 oil wells burning to our south, at our positions in northern Kuwait prevailing northerly winds had kept us relatively free from the plumes of smoke. On this day, though, southerly winds were carrying the black haze into Iraq. We were some 50 to 75 miles from the wells and still the sun was completely obscured. Like a thunderstorm rolling into the area, the clouds overhead were deep, black and threatening, but the rain from this storm never fell.

We came upon a paved highway with a major steel towered power line running alongside it. About 20 towers in a row had been toppled, with the cable lying on the ground. The story was that the Iraqis had toppled the power line with the idea of creating some type of electrical barrier. It hadn't worked. The toppled power lines stood like some modernistic scene of destruction wrought by our technically modern war machines. Along with the blackened sky and our own convoy of tanks and military equipment rolling through this part of the desert, the dark scene of devastation was complete.

Our convoy traveled along the highway, and soon met up with our new brigade. As we pulled into the brigade support area I saw fenced in circles of barbed wire holding Iraqi EPW's. Guarded by MP's with M-60 machine guns mounted atop humvees, the prisoners sat calmly. There were three or four of these circular areas with 10 or 20 shabbily dressed Iraqi soldiers in each. We drove to an open area and broke off with the rest of Headquarters company, making our now familiar circle formation. As the deuce-and-a-half I was riding in pulled into a slot next to a hemmit ammunition truck full of M1A1 main gun sabot rounds, the engine quieted and I listened for war. It was there, a far off distant thunder.

Chapter 19
Inferno

We did the typical things immediately upon our arrival; dig in. Since we were only 30 kilometers from the fighting in Basra, we were told that all sleeping arrangements, fighting positions, and trucks, would also be dug in. We were within reach of Iraqi artillery, so we dug our fighting position foxholes that first night. The next day an engineer unit showed up with a fancy army bulldozer and began digging in sleep positions for us. I put a cot in one of the holes; a three foot deep, six feet by six feet wide hole. I threw a piece of canvass tarp over the top and propped it in the middle with a pole and spreader (something we usually used for setting up camouflage netting). It wasn't half bad. I had enough room for my tools, bags, and equipment. In the end most guys didn't sleep in the holes, but since I presently had no vehicle to sleep in, I stayed in the hole. I kept guard in a hole during the day and slept in one at night.

I'd had a conversation with Sergeant Milano about this area of the world we were in. We were just south of the Tigris-Euphrates river valley; a place called Mesopotamia in ancient times, with the city of Babylon (not far from Baghdad) at its center. Sergeant Milano pointed out that this place was recognized as the beginning of known civilization. 5000 years ago the first organized cities had been formed here. In this place man left anarchy and formed governments. The earliest known uses of mathematics, accounting practices, and law were here. I was amazed that civilization could have started in such a desolate place. I have since learned that Mesopotamia had not always been so desolate. There had been fertile land and organized agricultural practices here. Over time the misuse of agriculture destroyed the land's fertility, rendering this place to desert. That ancient civilization destroyed its environment, its cities now lost.

The irony was not lost on me. Here we were with our modern machines, the most advanced weapons of war ever conceived, in a place as ancient as civilization, as old as supposed civilized warfare itself. I wondered how many wars had been waged on this same ground, how many countless battles, how many thousands perished? We were there again, repeating history.

Dump

Our main mission in coming back to this area was providing security for munitions teams as they blew the Iraqi munitions dump. The dump was incredible in size, measuring in square miles and containing about 200,000 tons of explosives. I didn't know if any of these were chemical weapons. The explosions which began rocking the area day and night told me it was mostly conventional material; no one would destroy chemical weapons by blowing them up directly, at least as long as they thought they were conventional. It was reported well after the end of the war that in other munitions dumps chemical weapons were destroyed by mistake. None of that occurred in this place, at least I never learned of such a thing in this area. By destroying these munitions we were keeping them out of the hands of the Republican Guard, which would surely use them against their own people in the battles around Basra.

In addition to the explosions at the dump just a few miles away, the distant rumble of war could be heard coming from Basra. Being in the holes we had dug would keep us a little safer if that Iraqi artillery turned on us. Though the cease fire with Iraq had held so far, we sure as hell didn't know if this would always be the case. With the remaining divisions of Hussein's Republican Guard less than 30 klicks from our position, we prepared for that possibility.

We were still taking EPW's at this point. I understood that some of these soldiers were picked up trying to retrieve munitions from the dump; others simply deserted because of the lack of food and water in the Iraqi Army. Most of these EPW's were taken to Saudi and placed in camps. Eventually they would be turned back to Iraq, which would probably be fatal for those that had deserted. They sat in the little fenced-in barbed wire circles all day waiting for transport from the area. As we drove by these areas on our daily radio maintenance runs I thought about the boredom of just sitting all day. Thoughts of boredom were becoming more common. Our job was beginning to be a waiting game.

We were in Iraq for six days and during most of that stay a dark purplish haze from the burning oil wells to our south darkened the skies. It was six days of sleeping in a three foot deep hole, being bolted from my sleep in the middle of the night by earth-shaking explosions from the munitions dump, and hearing war in the distance. The explosions in the middle of the night were most memorable. I was always sure we were under artillery attack when these occurred. Without a doubt those explosions moved the Richter scale.

After six days the place was secure enough for us to leave and head back into Kuwait to rejoin 1st Brigade. It was a clear day as we lined up to roll. The smoke had left and I think everyone felt pretty damn good about getting our of Iraq, even though all our backsides were a little bit sore. We'd gotten our Gammagobulin vaccine shots the day before. The vaccine kept us immune from every disease know to man the way I understood it. It was typical army medicine getting vaccinated in the desert; line up, drop your shorts, take the needle in your..... Even Sergeant T was in a pretty good mood. Often that hadn't been the case lately.

We took a different path back into Kuwait, traveling mostly on established roads. This was the first time since the war that we hadn't traveled in combat formation. Getting on a highway and traveling in convoy beat the hell out of driving in a rough desert. We traveled through many other units on our way back into Kuwait, including the U.S. 1st Armored Division and the British 1st Armored Division. There was VII Corps military everywhere we looked.

It took us a good part of the day to make the trip, all in all about 75 miles. As we crossed into Kuwait we hit tar roads and made excellent time. We were able to travel at 35 to 40 miles per hour, with the tanks and other track vehicles keeping up easily. As we rolled down the highway I noticed a white plume, steam it seemed, covering a great width of distance on the horizon. As we got closer I knew it was smoke from the oil well fires. After a few more miles I made out fiery orange flames shooting from the ground. As soon as I made out the first fire I was able to see more, then more, and more. Finally a fiery "hades" lay in front of our moving convoy, extending from one end of the horizon to the other. Not only did the fires stretch the width of the horizon, but went deep behind the first line of fires. As I was able to make out these blazing inferno's individually, I started to count; I lost track at 100. These were the Kuwaiti northern oil fields. Hundreds of wells burned here.

I was completely and totally astounded at what lay in front of me; amazed at the total and complete destruction. Oil storage tanks burned alongside these giant flamethrowers, torching the sky. No well was left untouched. Some spewed flames a hundred or two hundred feet high. Others seemed to burn in a low wide bushy manner; like the oil was spewing out in a wide gush, being consumed immediately by the voracious appetite of the all consuming flames. Some burned white smoke, others pitch black. Then I remembered the dream on New Year's Eve, the one at the USO in Frankfurt the day I was to leave for this place. I knew the furious, smoky blackness I had seen and felt in that dream lay here before me. Poor mother earth. Was it she who beckoned to me in my sleep that New Year's Eve night?

We continued down the asphalt highway, coming closer and closer to the inferno. At what seemed about two miles from the flames we came to a crossroads and made a left turn. As the road curved in front of us I saw Red Lion tanks traveling in a row stretching two to three miles. Destroyed tanks, civilian automobiles, and miscellaneous junk littered the desert to the sides of the convoy. It was like someone or something had picked up the burned military vehicles and junked cars and thrown them haphazardly across the dead brown desert sand. Every few miles a burned out building straddled the road we traveled.

We came upon an area that looked like it had been used for growing vegetable crops. Plots were laid out with built-up earthen walls surrounding them. With grass and some trees in the area, I could see this was a rare place indeed. With the right irrigation there was obviously some tillable land in this desert. We pulled into one of the earthen walled plots. Each walled area was about 1000 meters square; enough area to encamp our Headquarters company support team.

As the rest of the combat companies in the battalion headed to forward locations in the desert, Headquarters company broke off, setting up shop in our walled off plot. 1st Brigade, 3rd Armored Division lay all around us here, so we were not alone. After pulling into our area and settling in I looked out at the burning wells, the closest of which was about two miles distant. We were at the northern edge of the burning fields here and I immediately counted 30 or 40 wells in flames; these were ones I could clearly see. In the background were hundreds, just specks of orange light through the hellish haze. A northerly wind kept the area free from smoke that day; great plumes blew downwind in massive black columns. As everyone became settled and the engines from the trucks were stilled, I heard for the first time the roar of this inferno. Like a modern jet airport in the distance, the rumble was constant; the low pitched roar of a thousand massive torches. As the ground slightly trembled below us and the low dull roar of the flames billowed in the distance, I was surely seeing the fires of hell on earth.

Chapter 20
Safwan

March 22, 1991

Dear Family,

We just spent six days in Iraq blowing a huge munitions dump. We are now back in Kuwait camped about two to three miles from a huge burning oil field. We can hear the roar of the flames, like a jet airport in the distance. The ground shakes, literally, as when I sleep it rocks like a very slight quake! I have the feeling we are just on a sightseeing trip lately. If I didn't want to get the hell out of the desert so damn bad I'm sure I would be more than fascinated. So much destruction, you become numb and blase'. I have seen thousands of destroyed vehicles. We are on a main highway here with cars, trucks, and tanks blown apart and strewn to the side of the road. T-72 tanks destroyed and flipped on their tops. The dead have been mostly policed up. The border, though, between Iraq and Kuwait is very bad.

I feel the worst for the poor damn dogs left behind. Some are in packs looking for food. They won't last long here as the weather is getting warmer and drier. 80's in the day now - almost 90 sometimes. Nights are much nicer - 60's. We're supposed to shoot the dogs if they look threatening, though we just throw a rock. Some are dead along the roads. Strange to have more compassion for a dog than people.

Our front units were searching Bedouin camps for ammo holdouts in Iraq. Scared these people to death. Tanks pull right up to the tent, GI's walk in and search. People are starving. We can do nothing about this and nothing about his people killing each other. We must leave here. Our only other choice is to completely destroy the whole country if we want him. The American people do not realize what it will take or what it means to destroy a country. If we want to oust

174

Hussein we will have to occupy the government, fight warring factions, and occupy the country, probably for decades.

I'll end here. Have gone on enough! I don't know when we leave, only rumors. Some as short as 10 days - some say June. I go day to day! Will call soon.

Love

The Stars and Stripes reported that people wanted us to keep going. Let them come to this Godforsaken place and keep on going! I just wanted the hell out of the desert!

Over three weeks had passed since the ceasefire and for the first time in months we didn't have to dig in on our arrival back in Kuwait. We were now quite far from any Iraqis. There were still guards posted at the entrance to our company area and roving guards during the night hours. Stand-to was cut to just a roll-call in the morning, lessening the amount of guard duty we were pulling tremendously. Instead of having four hours of stand-to every day, plus one hour of gate guard and one hour of roving guard in the middle of the night, guard went down to one hour of roving guard in the middle of the night, every other night, and one hour of gate guard every other day. Not bad.

Sergeant T and I acquired a GP medium tent from the transportation platoon. A GP medium can sleep up to twenty GI's. Most of the GI's in maintenance still slept in their vehicles, but since Sergeant T and I now had no vehicle, we put up the tent. It was damn nice. We had so much room we were able to put a kitchen table (something we'd found from the household junk littering the area) in one corner of it. This made a good workbench and a nice place to store the radios that still came to us day in and day out. In another corner we'd dug a three foot square hole, three feet deep. We then threw a wooden packing crate over top of the hole, grabbed a bathroom sink we'd also acquired from the ransacked buildings in the area, then fashioned legs and a counter top for the sink. For privacy we took the million and one use rain poncho and fashioned a curtain around the area, thus giving us an honest to goodness half bath. With a five gallon bucket of water we had an effective shower.

Some of my comrades in maintenance became extremely creative, actually building a shower. The materials were simple: bricks for the floor; fiberglass sheeting for walls; and a small electric pump hooked up to a truck battery. A five gallon bucket of water was then placed next to the shower, with the hose from the pump sticking into the water. The pump pushed the water through half inch tubing to the top of the shower where a makeshift nozzle gave a pretty decent spray.

The cold water in those five gallon buckets was starting to feel pretty good. Temps were pushing into the 90's as April approached. Along with steadily warmer days, boredom began to set in hard. I was reading everything I could get my hands on. One day a buddy from the transportation platoon took a small rock, wrapped a hell of a lot of 100 mile an hour tape (army equivalent of duct tape, only green in color of course) around it, making an excellent softball. With a couple of bats and a few gloves from supply, we played softball every day for a couple of weeks (until the weather turned too warm). The rock in the ball would completely disintegrate on occasion, in which case we'd grab a new rock and tape another ball together. Supply set us up with a television and VCR hooked to a small generator. Somehow we'd acquired a bunch of movies, either from people at home or ones the supply platoon had thoughtfully thrown in. We'd sit around the supply tent after supper and watch the latest Rambo movie, or some such fare. The supply lines were improving so we received two hot meals everyday; breakfast and supper. The food wasn't bad, with real eggs for breakfast and chicken or steak sometimes for supper.

Enemy HQ

As April came the days began to creep by, slower and slower. We worked to keep ourselves busy, but found little to do much of the time. The medics and transportation platoons were beginning to pull real world assignments again as refugees from the fighting in Iraq flowed into our area. The trans guys had to haul food and water, the medics bandaged people up. In the meantime the rest of us had to find things to keep us busy.

One morning the trans platoon sergeant came by and asked if anyone in maintenance wanted to explore the Iraqi encampments and bunkers in the area. I gladly volunteered, and so Sergeant Wills and myself were off. Sergeant Wills was in his second war here. He'd been to Vietnam over 20 years earlier and was one of the few NCO's in the battalion with combat experience. He told pretty good stories about his experiences in Nam and I found myself in conversations with him often.

The encampments where Republican Guard troops had stayed were not far from where we had set up camp. Where previously the encampments I had seen were out in the desert, these were in the agricultural areas of this part of northern Kuwait. As we bounced down the rutted, dusty roads in Sergeant Wills' five ton truck, I took in the scene. A hot sun beat down from a cloudless blue sky on perfectly squared off plots of land, each I figured to be about ten acres. Green grass from the wet spring grew up around rusting irrigation equipment. Disrepaired farm machinery surrounded the warehouses and other buildings scattered throughout the area. Every square plot was separated by neatly laid out tree-lined roadways. None of the irrigation or farm equipment looked as if it had worked for some time. The occupation had stopped any farming in this area completely.

Our first stop was in a place with various warehouses and tool sheds. Sergeant Wills said he'd seen a lot of munitions during his first visit here and he wasn't kidding. In one small pumphouse we found hand grenades and other small explosives stacked to the ceiling. There were thousands of separate munitions, and all were marked with a Jordanian government seal on the outside of the boxes. "Government of Jordan" was on munitions boxes all over that area. As a matter of fact, I'd seen Jordanian government stamps on hundreds of munitions boxes since the ceasefire.

We traveled on, going from building to building and also to various dug-in bunkers in the area. The Republican Guard had apparently used this place for a headquarters. Some of the warehouses were laid out with offices, kitchens, and storage rooms which contained massive amounts of training books and other propaganda, all with Saddam Hussein's picture. I picked up some of the training books and a blue beret from a Republican Guard uniform for souvenirs. Berets were a hot item among GI's wanting souvenirs.

Some of the warehouses were used to house what seemed to be the offices of high ranking officers. In one of these warehouses we came upon a row of separated rooms and offices. As I stepped into one of the small bare rooms in this warehouse, I saw a bed in one corner with a dresser drawers and a mirror along the side wall. I opened the dresser drawers and found various womens toiletries; nail polish and the like. I looked into another corner where a pair of black, high heeled woman's shoes sat. I remember thinking how odd this seemed. What were a pair of woman's shoes doing in this place? Light shown into the room through red curtains, a red bedspread lay on the small single bed. In the room to the left of this bedroom was an office with desk and chairs; various official looking papers were strewn about. I was slowly putting two and two together as we walked into another small bare room to the right of the bedroom. Two steel metal folding chairs sat by themselves in the middle of this room. As Sergeant Wills and I rummaged through some propaganda books strewn on the floor in this odd little bare room, I kicked what I at first thought to be an animal fur of some kind. I kicked it again and I could see underlying dried skin.

"What the hell is that, Sarge?"

"Hmm." Sergeant Wills looked down and kicked the fur over again. As it rolled back over, my minds eye, which at first glance gave me a picture of animal fur, cleared. I saw straight, thick black human hair; woman's hair. "It's a scalp," Sergeant Wills said, his voice void of any emotion.

I looked down. Again I saw the flaking dried skin on the underside of the hair. The complete picture of what this place was crashed into my brain. A brief picture of the horror that had occurred here rocked my senses .... At that moment, did I know that for the rest of my life I would turn that hair over and over in my mind, a thousand times since that day, and question what I saw; that I would wonder who this woman was and how she became entrapped in such evil; that I would wonder if she was beautiful, and did her family still search for her? I can't remember all my thoughts, though I refused to believe what I saw in that room for a very long period of time. I now know that what I saw was reality. It had really happened ....

I looked over at Sergeant Wills while we were still in the room. He'd turned away, silently thumbing through an Iraqi military manual. I looked down at one of the manual's I'd picked up, Saddam smiled back from the cover. Sergeant Wills walked out of the room in silence and I followed, looking back one more time.

As we climbed into the five ton and drove out of this place my mind reconnected, over and over, the separate images I'd just seen. Sickness swept through me as I pictured the violence of torture; the horror of mans inhumanity to man ....

As a high school student I researched Hitler's attempted genocide of the Jewish race. I can't forget the feeling I had in first reading, then picturing the hundreds of thousands, and millions killed. This realization shocked and sickened me to my core. I visited Dachau Concentration Camp outside of Munich, Germany the second year of my tour there. The moment I walked through the gates of that camp a chill started up my spine, ending with a tingling sensation at the back of my head. I could literally feel what had happened in this place.

I saw the ovens. I stood looking out a window in a room attached to that oven room. As I turned to look away from that window, my eyes fell upon a life size photograph hung on an adjacent wall, taken from the exact spot I stood looking out that window. The emaciated bodies of dead Jews piled four feet deep lay in front of that window. It had really happened ....

This same type of unleashed sickness had occurred at that warehouse. These were war crimes; crimes against humanity. Evil exists. Have no doubt.

I thought about the swift justice of an M-1A1, 120mm sabot round. Some of the perpetrators of the evil in this place had found this swift justice, and I have no qualms in having helped provide it. For the rest, justice has yet to be dispensed.

Bouncing in the truck back to the company area, I looked over at Sergeant Wills' road-map face, covered with dust from the dry roads we were traveling. He was a hard-core vet who had seen things in Vietnam that made the last few months here a cakewalk. He once told me a story that his company had been attacked by a North Vietnamese Regular Army battalion. He'd fired an M-60 machine gun at the on-coming NVA through a whole night, the barrel of the machine gun glowing red and then white. He could literally see the bullets travelling down the white hot translucent barrell. The bodies were piled on top of each other in the morning. He'd lived to tell about it.

Refugees

As the conflict between the Shiite Moslems of southern Iraq and the remnants of Hussein's Guard troops raged north of us, the human tide of refugees began to make its presence felt in the extreme south of Iraq. Our present position in Kuwait was approximately ten kilometers south of the town of Safwan, Iraq. Elements of the Red Lions stretched from my position with Headquarters company some ten klicks into Kuwait. From there it went north to Safwan and beyond. A twelve mile wide demilitarized zone had been set up, straddling the border six miles deep on either side. The area was basically a safe haven for those Iraqis fleeing the fighting in Basra and other cities.

It was in the town of Safwan that a refugee camp was set up for the flow of people. The camp was run by elements of my First Bri-gade, 3rd Armored, with the main control and administration by us in the Red Lions. It was Red Lion medics who worked at the camp every day and Red Lion transportation platoon guys who, along with others in the brigade, hauled food and water in every day. By the end of April, 25,000 Iraqi Shiite refugees were in the camp at Safwan. Some came because their homes had been destroyed, most though, were fleeing because they had supported the failing attempt to overthrow Hussein. Their lives and their families' lives were in great danger. Their only safe haven was this US protected DMZ.

This was later called the humanitarian side of our mission. When the speeches by generals were made later, they called us not only good soldiers who did their duty, but compassionate soldiers as well. If people came they were given shelter, food, and water. As the camp filled, medics and trans guys were coming back to the company area talking about the barefoot kids, their feet bleeding from the journey to Safwan, and families almost starved for lack of food. Children who had picked up unexploded munitions were losing fingers, hands, or their lives. Cluster bombs dropped by the multiple launch rockets were everywhere. The little baseball size bomblets were just the right size for curious kids to pick up. If the bomblets did not explode immediately, the kids sometimes took them into homes where some went off, killing or maiming other members of the family. My buddies, the medics of the Red Lions, were getting a real taste of the aftermath of war. Families, women and children, were victims of the leftovers lying everywhere around the countryside. EOD teams (demolitions) worked day in and day out blowing the unexploded munitions. Two teams worked a five mile radius around Safwan. Every day for two months they blew munitions. They would never get it all.

May 3, 1991

Dear Adrienne,

I am still in northern Kuwait. It has been a terribly long and boring ordeal here. My unit is supporting the refugees at Safwan, Iraq. There are about 30,000 there and is an unbelievable sight; a massive tent city. We truck food and water to them daily, and provide security and medical aid. I could be extremely vivid in my account of this I suppose. It is more intense then anything I have experienced here so far.

I guess the children affect me the most. With their dark complexion these are outwardly very beautiful people, the children especially. Even in such a miserable existence the kids in the camps play and are always happy to see GI's. We travel through the villages and countryside, kids come up to the vehicle wanting to trade things. They offer us Iraqi money (dinars) for MRE's or cigarettes. The town of Safwan is an experience in itself. We walk through the market areas and talk, as best we can, to the vendors selling onions, tomatoes, and trinkets on the sidewalks. The market on the streets of Safwan is as old as civilization itself. My mind's eye seems to recognize it as unchanged through thousands of years, hundreds of generations. The smells and activity transport me back in time.

The towns and cities of this part of Iraq are almost completely destroyed. The town of Safwan is shot to hell. The main street is riddled with bullet-pocked walls and burned-out, overturned autos. Yet life here has a feel of normalcy. The kids go to school. There is as yet no electricity, but the modern conveniences destroyed by the war have not made day to day living lose a step. Maybe this ancient culture has seen innumerable times like this. People in southern Iraq seem extremely happy that we are here. Signs saying "Free us from Saddam's bloodmen" and "No For Saddam" are painted all over the town of Safwan.

Immediately after the ceasefire when the Shiite Moslems of southern Iraq rebelled, Saddam and the remnants of his Republican Guard crushed the revolt, purging those taking part, in some areas killing all males over the age of 15. When we leave I do not know what will happen to those people of Safwan who Saddam feels may have risen against him. There is great fear here. I must feel that fear also.

Love

Carey

183

Chapter 21
EOD

As the oil fires raged, giving us a light show in the evenings worse than any picture of hell, we went on with our mission. On two different days I traveled with an EOD (Explosives Ordinance and Demolition) team into and around the town of Safwan. We traveled with an army interpreter, going into the market area of Safwan to ask people if they knew of unexploded munitions. On our first trip into town we stopped at the small hospital, staffed mostly with US Army physicians, set up to treat local people and the refugees flowing into the area from the ravaged southern part of Iraq. One of the doctors knew of people who could tell us where munitions were and directed us to them. As we left the hospital, a little Iraqi boy grabbed and hugged one of the MP's traveling with us. This routine had been repeated many times and the boy and the MP had become friends. I noticed townsfolk around us staring. I suppose it was an unusual sight, the boy hugging this US Army soldier.

We came upon our first set of cluster bombs just outside the town. They had been marked with a sign in Arabic telling of the danger. They were blown quickly. At our next site I could see the bomblets had been moved and placed side by side in one spot. Any movement can set off a cluster bomb. The people who'd moved these must have been living right.

We used C-4 to destroy these bomblets. As we unloaded a box of the explosive, one of the EOD guys grabbed a block of this plastic Styrofoam type material and slapped it against my chest. He laughed and the rest of the EOD guys gave me a hard time because I jumped a foot. When I saw the C-4 coming at me I thought it was all over. The stuff is really inert until a blasting cap is inserted into the material. A small electrical charge from a hand-pumped detonator box travels through wire to the blasting cap, setting it and the C-4 off; just like in the movies. Since I had no hole in my chest I guess I'm living proof that by itself C-4 is fairly harmless; I don't recommend pushing the theory, though.

Traveling on through the countryside we stopped at a small mudhif (mud house) where we had been told there were bombs nearby. Two young women came out of the house with two or three young children. Both women were probably in their twenties. The younger of the two had a very dark, exotic Persian look about her. Even in a shabby dirty dress, her beauty was inescapable. I thought she was strikingly attractive; of course, being in the desert for four months had enhanced my appreciation of a beautiful woman.

The older of the two women signaled for cigarettes so one of the MP's hurried over to her, happily handing her a few Marlboro's. I looked over again at the younger woman, who caught my eye at the same instant, and with a seductive look she began licking her lips repeatedly. The interpreter, sitting next to me, caught her look immediately and nudged me saying "Hey, man. That woman wants you!"

"I'm getting the same feeling," I said, never taking my eyes away from hers. I'd have had to be a dead man not to pick up on the look she was giving me. The woman oozed sensuality.

"It's an Arabic custom, man!" the interpreter kept on. "A woman licking her lips means she's yours. Sex, man! Pussy!"

The interpreter didn't have to tell me the customs. The looks we were giving each other would melt polar ice, they needed no interpreter. We had instant communication! No language barrier existed between us whatsoever. As she smiled at me, batting her dark eyes and licking full sensuous lips, pictures of half naked Persian belly dancers coursed through my brain. I concentrated on her soft, dark features, and it was her, in a low hip hugging skirt, swaying deliciously in front of me. Allah! We continued to stare at one another for what seemed like hours. Time really does stop! I drank in all she could give me from her eyes .... It was probably just a minute later that everyone loaded into the hummers and we roared off, the young woman and I staring at each other unflinchingly until we were gone. The interpreter thought the situation was fascinating. He kept nudging me, telling me I could have had the woman. Yes, I could have. The only problem I could see in figuring how I could have her was the fact that she lived in a demilitarized zone. I would steal a vehicle in the middle of the night, drive over an international border while crossing through at least three military checkpoints. If I got through the M-16 carrying troops and the M-1 tanks, she was mine!

Even though our base camp in northern Kuwait was only 30 klicks or so from Safwan, it was another country and a world away. It wasn't like we ever had free time, even after the ceasefire was called. We were on constant wartime footing with guard duty around the clock. In old war movies about Vietnam, and even some about WW II, I saw GI's getting time off to go into the nearest town to get drunk and meet the local women. Maybe that was just the movies. I suppose most of the poor bastards in those wars got about as much time off as I did in this one. None.

I thought about the encounter with the young woman a lot after it happened; visions of this Persian beauty danced in my head for a long time; a long time! I'd read a book on Iraqi culture a buddy of mine's sister had sent from the States. Most people have the idea that all Arabic women wear veils and are completely obedient to their men. This is mostly true of women who have men. For a woman who had never been married, promiscuity before her marriage can be a death sentence. A passage from the book told of a wedding ceremony where immediately after the marriage vows the couple went into the bed chamber, where a clean white sheet had been laid on the bed. The husband made love to his new wife right then and there while the relatives waited in the outside room! When the young man emerged from the bed chamber he was smiling and this meant everything was acceptable (if he'd been unhappy, this was another thing). The related women then ran into the bedroom to inspect the sheet. A bloodied sheet marked the woman a virgin and meant the marriage was a good one. If the woman had not been a virgin, the groom could have requested that the girl's family have her killed.

There were few men among the people I observed around Safwan. Most it seemed had been killed in the war or later in the uprising. There were no men at this house and it seemed both women had probably lost husbands. It seemed there was no taboo at all about promiscuity after the loss of a husband.

We found other munitions not far from the mudhif with the two women. The EOD guys were real pros and efficiently blew the bomblets we'd found. I wondered about these guys as we traveled from place to place that day. I got into a couple of conversations with a few of them and they talked about blowing things up when they were kids; things like tree houses, small bridges out in the country, and the like. One guy said he'd had a chemistry set and had manufactured high explosives in his basement. Yes, most of these guys were a danger to society. Thank God the army had found them a job.

At one point that afternoon we stopped outside Safwan to look at a map. Soon a bunch of kids from the area were all over our humvee. They pronounced "MRE" and asked for cigarettes. I gave one of them an MRE but wouldn't give them cigarettes. Supposedly their parents had put them up to asking us for cigarettes, at least that's what the interpreter said they were telling us. I noticed their clothing, as most wore the single tunic. Some were white, others of different colors, all were dirty. It was over 100 degrees that day and I wondered how they stood the hot sand under their bare feet.

I noticed one little girl who stood out from the rest. She was six or seven years old and wore a pretty flowered tunic. She was a beautiful child with straggly brown hair and a light complexion. I gave here a cookie bar from an MRE pack and then she stepped back to watch the boys who were dealing with the EOD guys over cigarettes and Iraqi dinars with Hussein's picture (a truly hot item when it was thought Hussein would be taken out of power). I looked back at this child who stood out like a beacon amid the devastation around her. The contrast between her beauty and the surrounding ugliness was shattering. Her quizzical innocence struck me deeply. Talk to any GI who took care of those refugees and it was the kids who busted them up. I stepped out of the vehicle to take her picture. I wanted to remember this child in the pretty flowered dress and the dirty bare feet.

As evening approached we called it a day and started our trip back through the various checkpoints around Safwan, to the Kuwaiti side of the border and our temporary home. The guy driving the hummer was a young buck sergeant from battalion staff who was already in his second war. He'd been to Panama one year earlier in that little thing with Manuel Noriega. I asked him if he thought he wasn't pushing his luck being in two wars in one year's time. He grunted something about getting the hell out of the army.

It was a 20 or 30 klick drive back to our assembly area and I watched the sun hit the horizon. An orange red hue descended over the cooling desert, shimmering still from the heat that day. As we drove the radio carried chatter back and forth between various Red Lion units manning checkpoints around Safwan. The chatter, usually background noise, gained my attention.

"Red Lion six. Red Lion six. This is alpha checkpoint, over."

"Yeah, alpha checkpoint, this is six, go ahead."

"Ahh, six, this is alpha checkpoint. We need a message relayed to band-aid (medics). Jesus, sir, we got a little girl here picked up a bomblet of some type. She's got fingers blown off. We need band-aid down here ASAP."

"Alpha checkpoint, this is band-aid. We copied that. Ahh, on our way."

"Roger, band-aid."

As the dust flew behind us and the wind tore through our moving vehicle, I watched the sun, a deep dark red now, as it sunk below the horizon.

"Hey 'J', you got gate guard, man. Dudley's up there yelling for someone to replace him."

"I'm not supposed to have it until tonight. You must have looked at the list wrong."

"No way. They changed it this morning. Didn't you look?"

"Shit. They should have said something, man." I stepped out of the tent we'd set up for recreation in our company area. We had some board games in there with the TV and VCR. It was at least 105 degrees that day. The heat was starting to hit us really hard. I grabbed all my gear and headed for the gate. Dudley was there to meet me.

"Goddamnit 'J'. You knew you had this shit. How come your late?"

"It's only ten minutes, 'D'. They changed the list this morning. I wasn't supposed to be on till tonight."

"You should look at the goddamn list everyday, man. You get pissed as hell when nobody shows up to replace you! You piss me off, 'J'!

"Damn, 'D'. I'll make it up to you, man." Dudley just walked away. I turned and watched him pace back to the tent. Jesus, we'd been in the desert a long time. The weeks and now months were going by one after the other and only rumor as to when we'd get the hell out. And the heat. It was over 100 degrees every day now. I had to take a liter of water with me to the guard shack. Something was eating at 'D' because I'd never seen him go off before. I guess this shit would get to anybody. Not only the heat, but the wind blows all the goddamn time. Sand sticks to the sweat on my face. Sand is in my ears and in my eyes; and the flies, they're everywhere. We get our food and the flies attack. I have to fight the little bastards for my chow.

I did my two hour shift at the gate that afternoon; slugged down a lot of water; passed the time with a cheap novel. Days were incredibly monotonous so I read any old trashy thing I could find. This was some romance novel, one of those you see in the supermarket checkout aisle. Had a picture on the cover with a man and a woman in a passionate embrace. I don't remember the story at all, now. After my shift I walked back to our maintenance tent. The hot sun at my back and the roaring oil wells to my front. I wondered if those torches from hell added to the unreal heat. No doubt. The smoke billowing from them was incredible. The wind blew it away from us most of the time, but about once a week or so the wind shifted and we got hit for about a day. Thick putrid haze that I could taste and feel in my lungs.

I walked into the tent and threw my gear in a corner. It was toward evening suppertime. I laid back on my cot and started back into the trashy novel. Williams, a guy from the mortar platoon, stuck his head into the tent. He was supposed to have been discharged and had even gotten orders to fly, but he'd been held up and was now living with us in the maintenance tent. He was one of the guys held over when Hussein invaded Kuwait. They gave him an indefinite end of service date and sent him to the desert. He'd been living for over a month in the maintenance tent and we'd gotten along well. He was from California, a well-read dude whose sister had sent the book on Iraqi culture with the story about the marriage party. I looked up from the trashy novel. "What's up?"

"Did you hear the news, Jonesey?"

"No, man. What is it?"

"You know Sergeant Summerall from Charlie company?"

"Yeah, sure. He was ...." I stopped. I knew exactly what his next words would be.

"He was killed today, man. Stepped on a cluster bomb."

I stared at Williams for a minute, then rolled my feet over the edge of the cot. I stared at the imprints my combat boots made in the sand. V-shaped lines. Unconnected. I flashed back to the day at the NCO Academy when my former instructor talked about his life, and about dying. He bore his soul completely to us that day. I thought he'd done that to teach us something, something about compassion maybe. Now, I didn't know. Maybe that day was for some other purpose .... I felt an odd understanding, then. The knowledge and the heat in the tent pushed into my awareness. That familiar, tingly adrenaline rush enveloped my scalp, traveling to may face; though fear was not the cause this time. "How'd it happen?"

"I guess he and his tank crew stopped by the side of the road to investigate some cluster bombs. His crew said he was showing them how not to get killed by one of those little fuckers, then he tripped or kicked one. It tore off his legs, got his guts real bad. I guess the goddamn medivac chopper took thirty minutes. He was pretty bad, though. Lost too much blood."

"Christ, he knew the cluster bombs could get your ass killed. Everybody knows that .... It doesn't make any sense, man."

"That's the story, Jonesey."

"Yeah." I got up and walked to the door of the tent. I looked out at the scene from hell as it raged on, its fury expressing what I felt. There was no expression from me, though. I could find none. I turned back to see Williams in his cot staring into some cheap novel of his own. "It's my birthday today, man."

"Happy birthday, Jonesey."

Epilogue

I boarded a jet back to Germany, along with the rest of the Red Lions, on 20 May, 1991. Just two days before the temperature had reached 118 degrees. That night we slept under the stars as all vehicles and tents had gone to storage that afternoon. The temperature never fell below 100 that night, then the wind started. Blowing sand and sweat had caked my eyes closed by morning.

There are lots of bits and pieces of events that come to mind after writing this. Many I've gone back to put into the text, others will be in another story. Before we left northern Kuwait and the Safwan region most of the 25000 Shiite refugees, household belongings with farm animals included, were flown by C-130 transport planes to a refugee camp in Rafha, Saudi Arabia. By late 1992 a resettlement program had brought 3000 to the United States, 6000 to Iran, and 750 to Sweden. At that time there were still 26000 Iraqi Shiites, including captured Iraqi soldiers who refused to return to Iraq, in the refugee camps at Rafha.

After we returned to Germany I watched with interest the progress in putting out the oil well fires. Before the year 1991 ended all 900 plus fires were extinguished, two years ahead of the most pessimistic projections.

With the collapse of the Soviet Union in late 1991, adding to the string of world-altering events during those years, never before in history has so much power now resided with one nation. The one overwhelming impression this experience has left me with is the feeling of awe and terror at seeing the use of that power. General George

Patton talked about glory and war, and I guess it's glorious if you win. I've talked to a lot of Vietnam vets since I returned. An excellent book on the subject is *Vietnam: Our Story, One On One,* a collection of true stories compiled by Gary D. Gullickson, a Vietnam vet from my home town. Gary read this manuscript and gave me encouragement to keep going. The Vietnam vets stories are different, except the talk about destruction, and the kids. Another vet from my hometown, Kenny, who served in Nam, sat down with me when I first came home. He'd read a letter I'd written to my hometown paper in which I'd talked about the kids (this was actually part of the letter I'd written to Adrienne in chapter 21). He told me how he still remembered the kids he'd seen in Nam. We both cried talking about the kids.

I wrote to my sister after the war and told her now that I had seen war I had to work for peace. I haven't figured out yet how to do this. Maybe the Peace Corps, or maybe just trying to be a gentle human being (though I often fail at this pursuit miserably). We would all generate a lot of peace if we could just find this one attribute.

Finally, I believe there is a certain fabric to the future, and even time itself, which is set in a way, but on the other hand can be completely altered. If we are knowledgeable of those things which could occur we can, without doubt, change or control them. Please indulge me just a little and read a summation of the words of the French writer Nostradamus. Nostradamus wrote, and this was hundreds of years ago, that the two nations of the Arctic pole would someday unite to defeat a Persian warlord. In the uniting of these two great nations the world would then see a peace, the kind of which it has never known.

Thank you.

194

In memory of the 4-32 AR soldiers
who made the ultimate sacrifice.

PFC Adrian Leonard StokesSSG Roy Junior Summerall
SSG Christopher Stephens

WHY DO GOOD GUYS HAVE TO DIE

WHILE WELLS OF OIL BURN IN FLAME
THE DISTANT GLOW JUST ISN'T THE SAME
IT ONCE WAS FUN TO STARE AFAR
AND WISH UPON OUR FAVORITE STAR
BUT NOW THAT STAR COULD BE AN EYE
A FRIEND, A MAN, A SPECIAL GUY
WE KNEW THIS MAN FROM MOMENTS PAST
BUT THEN WE THOUGHT THE TIMES WOULD LAST
WE CAME SO FAR ON DREAMS ALONE
AND PRAYED OUR PRAYERS OF GOING HOME
WE FOUGHT EACH MILE GAINING GROUND
AND NEVER ONCE BACKING DOWN
THROUGH WIND, RAIN, AND ENEMY FIRE
THE COALITION REFUSED TO TIRE
WE GAVE UP SLEEP AND MEALS TOO
FOR MOST OF US WE MADE IT THROUGH
WE LEARNED THAT WAR IS NOT A GAME
AND NEVER SEEMS TO FIGHT THE SAME
WE ALSO LEARNED YOU HUNKER DOWN
AND WHEN IT'S OVER WATCH YOUR GROUND
WE THOUGHT IT WAS SAFE TO WONDER STRAY
BUT NOW OUR FRIEND HAS PASSED AWAY
WHY DO GOOD GUYS HAVE TO DIE?
I HAVE NO ANSWER, JUST GOODBYE!

Written by
Jon Rowland

Jon Rowland was a crewmember in Sgt. Summerall's M1A1 tank.